PAUL BOCUSE

MY CLASSIC CUISINE

Paul Bocuse

My Classic Cuisine

PYRAMID BOOKS

Acknowledgments

Editor Diana Craig
Art editors Sue Rawkins, Bob Gordon
Copy editor Rosamond Man
Production controller Alyssum Ross

Photographs pages 14, 15, 56, 57, 134, 135 & 148 James Murphy
Photograph page 152 Paul Webster

Originally published in Germany in 1988
by Zabert Sandmann Verlag GmbH under
the title *Paul Bocuse: Mein Meisterwerk*

First published in Great Britain in 1989
by Pyramid
an imprint of the Octopus Publishing Group
Michelin House
81 Fulham Road
London SW3 6RB

ISBN 1 871307 68 6

Produced by Mandarin Offset
Printed and bound in Hong Kong

CONTENTS

Introduction

'For me, cookery doesn't mean caviar, pâté de foie gras and truffles. To cook well, you don't necessarily have to have expensive produce. As a cook, what you should be doing is bringing out the full flavour of the products.' So speaks Paul Bocuse. It is a statement which may surprise many, especially those who remember him chiefly for his 'Elysée truffle soup'. But it is not such a contradiction.

That was a dish created for a very special dinner, held at the Elysée Palace to celebrate the award to Paul Bocuse of the *Légion d'Honneur*, for his services to French cuisine. For such an occasion, there must be a touch of grandeur, reflected, in that instance, by the inclusion of fresh truffles – the delicacy most highly prized by gourmets. Consider, though, the simplicity of the dish: a light chicken consommé, served in deep bowls, a few diced carrots, onions, mushrooms, the truffles, naturally, and also a little foie gras on that occasion, topped with a puff pastry lid. As you break into the pastry, a wonderful aroma wafts out. Truffles, of course, have a particularly powerful scent - but the idea is superbly simple, and one which is easily translated into humbler ingredients, to just as good effect. That is the essence of Bocuse. Simple ideas, a not-over-elaborate presentation, and always top-quality, though not necessarily expensive, products.

In France, this passion for fresh produce is synonymous with the name of Bocuse. He is famed for his daily walks through the market in Lyons, seeking out the plumpest chickens from Bresse, the tenderest, young spinach leaves , the best artichokes, the freshest goat cheeses. He wanders amongst the stalls, eyes darting everywhere – looking, feeling, sniffing. Only at the end of the shopping expedition, on his return to the restaurant at Collonges-au-Mont-d'Or on the outskirts of the city, does the menu for that day's luncheon take shape. It is a very French attitude, of course and an age-old tradition. For Paul Bocuse, particularly so, since he is the twelfth generation of his family to be a chef, still in the same village which, in 1725, provided his ancestor with *his* first customers. Now, they fly in from all over the world – from Spain for Lunch, from London for dinner, chefs from all over France. Some have been his apprentices, now they have their own Michelin-starred restaurants, for Bocuse is as generous with his talent as he is proud of it.

His own grounding was impeccable. After the Second World War, during which he fought for the Free French, he spent the next fourteen years at three three-star establishments: La Mère Brazier, outside Lyons; La Pyramide, at Vienne, under Fernand Point – then France's most renowned and creative chef; finally, at Lucas-Carton, Lapérouse. It paid off. Succeeding his father at Collonges in 1959, within seven years he had his own three stars. He loves French cooking, and is committed to spreading its gospel. But always, he remembers the ordinary man- and woman-in-the-street, the cook at home in his or her own kitchen. 'You have to cook the cookery of the people. This is cookery that everyone can understand'.

FISH AND SHELLFISH

MANY OF THE FINEST DISHES ON THE MENUS of restaurants in France
— be they *haute cuisine* establishments or simple village inns —
involve fish or seafood. And it does not necessarily follow that because
a restaurant is three-starred and expensive, the fish will be one of the
'grander' species. 'It is a mistake if people today believe that the most
expensive fish are also the best. Certainly there are around three kings
among sea fish — the turbot, the sea bass and the angler. But we forget
too readily that the simpler fish also include some delicious varieties. I
am particularly fond of skate, and of course the incomparable herring.
Fish from the cold Northern waters are generally of excellent quality.
I would prefer any fish from the North to a Mediterranean fish. Of all
the freshwater fish, the one I like best is the carp. A wonderful fish.
Cooked quite simply in the oven with red wine, or cut into rounds
and grilled, carp are at their best in winter, when the water is colder
and cleaner. Pike has a great tradition in our family. We eat it at
weddings and first communions. For all fish, the rule is the same:
cook it for as little time and as gently as possible.'

In a dozen or so sentences, Bocuse has encompassed the French
attitude to fish. Centuries ago, other European countries, under
French influence, shared this attitude, too. Every monastery, and
most of the manor houses, had their own carp pond, often stocked
with several hundred fish. They had many mouths to feed, of course,
and several fast days each week: on Tuesday and Saturday, as well as
the better-remembered Friday, no meat was allowed. The volume of
fish thus consumed was enormous and, if the diet was not to be
monotonous, the cook not only had to be imaginative with his recipes
but to use as many varieties of fish as he could find. From streams and
rivers came grayling, char, whitefish, trout, pike, perch, and eels too.
The pike, so beloved of early anglers, can sometimes be ordered from
the fishmonger, but for the 'daynteous and holsom' perch, the
delicate grayling and char, you have to don wellingtons, pick up the
rod and fish it yourself. As for the carp, their ponds have long
disappeared, though appreciation for that firm sweet flesh seems to be
returning and one can see the brightly scaled fish more often today —
although they may not be native produce. A couple of those
gleaming scales, incidentally, tucked into the purse, would ensure
prosperity for the year to come — so the ancients said. Perhaps we
should revive that tradition, take a lead from Bocuse, and bring the
carp back into fashion.

Maybe Oliver Cromwell should shoulder some of the blame for the lack of fish on our plates. For with his abolishment of fast days came devastation to the fishing industry, and the prejudice aroused then still lingers on.

The French do not have this prejudice, they do not believe that just because they do not live by the sea, they should not enjoy the sea's bounty, and almost every town, however small, however far inland, will have a stall with beautifully fresh fish for sale at least once a week. Bass and monkfish, of course, are deservedly popular – if not cheap (though the French have few reservations about paying as much for fish as for meat), but so too, as Bocuse says, are skate (for that classic, *raie au beurre noir*), and 'the incomparable herring'.

Skate is an ideal traveller, since it is one of the few fish best eaten at least twelve hours after capture. Only then will the gelatinous coating be easy to rinse off, and the flavour matured. Herrings, on the other hand, must be bought fine, fat and very fresh. But, salted with spices, they keep wonderfully and, soaked in fruity olive oil, provide that favourite of French starters, *filets d'harengs*. From such humble beginnings, though, can come great dishes: Bocuse salts his herrings, then vividly presents them in a beetroot juice aspic set on a fresh herb sauce. A brilliant dish – both in its contrast of colours, and of tastes.

For the romantically named 'fruits of the sea', however, Bocuse recommends simplicity. The lobster, the langoustine, mussel and scallop should all be 'eaten as naturally as possible'– which is fitting for creatures of such delicate but distinctive flavour. Such delicacy, though (with the thankful exception of the mussel), is sadly expensive, insisting that it be celebratory food – all too often extravagantly presented, over-spiced and over-sauced. Bocuse keeps his seafood marriages simple: a little curry powder for the sweetness of the mussel; sorrel as a foil for the even sweeter scallop. For the lobster he reserves a masterly touch – a match with one of summer's other great luxuries: fresh young peas, puréed to a light frothy soup. Decidedly elegant.

The mark of a great cook is confidence in simplicity. Even more so is restraint, and for the king of the 'sea fruits' – the oyster – Bocuse will give no recipe. 'Oysters should not be heated or adulterated by preparations of any kind. They should simply be served in their own liquid. That is the best for the oyster.' Some things no cook can improve upon. An oyster *au naturel* is one of them.

PERCH FILLETS IN BEER BATTER
FILETS DE PERCHE FRITS DANS UNE PÂTE À LA BIÈRE

Serves 4
1 litre (1¾ pints) vegetable oil
sea salt
450 g (1 lb) fillets of perch (one of the most delicious freshwater fish, much used on the Continent: if necessary, substitute pike or a really fresh sea-water fish such as cod or haddock)

1–2 tablespoons flour
1 bunch curly parsley

For the beer batter:
200 g (7 oz) flour
2 egg yolks
250 ml (9 fl oz) beer
pinch of salt
pinch of sugar
40 g (1½ oz) butter, melted
2 egg whites

For the lemon sauce:
4 shallots, finely chopped
125 ml (4 fl oz) white wine
2 tablespoons dry vermouth
1 tablespoon lemon juice
½ teaspoon tarragon vinegar
125 g (4 oz) butter, chilled and diced
sea salt
freshly ground black pepper

For the batter, sift the flour into a large bowl, add the egg yolks and beer and whisk vigorously until smooth. Or simply whizz all together in a food processor. Stir in the salt, sugar and melted butter, then leave to stand for 30 minutes at room temperature.

Beat the egg whites to a light froth, and carefully fold into the batter.

To make the lemon sauce, cook the shallots in the wine and vermouth until the liquid has evaporated and the shallots are soft and mushy. Add the lemon juice and vinegar, then beat in the butter, a knob at a time, making sure each piece is quite absorbed before adding the next. Adjust the seasoning and keep warm.

Heat the oil in a pan or deep fat fryer to about 180 °C/350°F, (a cube of stale bread will brown in 60 seconds). Salt the fish fillets, coat with flour, shaking off excess, then whisk the batter briskly and dip in the fish into it to coat thoroughly. Cook in the hot oil for about 2 minutes, until golden brown, turn over and cook the other side briefly.

Transfer on to kitchen towel to drain off excess fat. Then add the parsley to the oil and fry very briefly until crisp, but take care not to burn it. Also stand well back when adding the parsley as it will splutter. Divide the lemon sauce between four plates, place the fish on top and garnish with parsley.

First coat the seasoned fillets in flour, then dip into the beer batter

Drain off any surplus batter and add the fillets to the hot oil

*To accompany, try a distinctive dry white wine from the Loire, such
as Sancerre or Jasnières*

Once the first side is golden brown,
turn over carefully, and cook the other
side briefly

Transfer the fish on to kitchen towel to
absorb excess fat

BRAISED CARP
CARPE BRAISÉE

Serves 4

2 small carp, each about 1 kg (2 lbs),
cleaned, scaled, then cut in half
lengthways (i.e. from the back down
to the belly)
25 g (1 oz) butter
sea salt
freshly ground black pepper
For the herb stuffing:
150 g (5 oz) fresh white bread, crusts
removed, grated into breadcrumbs
125 g (4 oz) butter, softened
2 tablespoons finely chopped basil
leaves
2 tablespoons finely chopped chervil
leaves
3 tablespoons finely chopped parsley
sea salt
freshly ground black pepper
For the lemon butter:
1 lemon
100 g (3½ oz) butter
4 tablespoons reduced veal stock (page
150)
sea salt
freshly ground black pepper

Place the fish in a large dish, cover with iced water and leave in the refrigerator up to 24 hours. Drain and pat dry with kitchen towel. Butter a large baking sheet (or two if necessary), sprinkle with salt and pepper and lay the carp halves on top. Season lightly with salt and pepper.

To make the stuffing, mix the breadcrumbs in the softened butter, then stir in the herbs. Season with salt and pepper and spread evenly over the fish, leaving the heads and tails exposed.

Cook for about 20 minutes in the oven, preheated to 220°C/425°F/gas 7, until the flesh is firm and opaque. Check after 10–15 minutes and, if necessary, cover with greaseproof paper or foil to prevent the top from burning.

To make the lemon butter, peel the lemon, removing all the white pith, then divide into segments, skinning them over a bowl to catch any juice. Squeeze out juice from the skins then set segments aside.

Heat the butter until foaming, pour through a fine sieve, return to the pan and brown lightly. Moisten with the lemon juice, stir in the veal stock, adjust the seasoning and add the lemon segments just to heat through.

Remove the carp from the oven. Cut off the heads and tails, then carefully ease the fillets off the bones. Divide each fillet into two and serve on a pool of lemon butter.

Lay the halved carp on a buttered, seasoned baking sheet. Season

Cover with the herb stuffing, leaving the head and tail of the fish exposed

*To accompany, try a full-bodied dry white wine, such as an Alsace
Pinot Gris or an old-style white Rioja (Marqués de Murrieta, and
CUNE's Monopole are good examples)*

Smooth the stuffing evenly all over with
a knife

Cook for approximately 20 minutes in
the oven, preheated to 220 °C/425°F/
gas 7. To serve, cut off head and tail,
and carefully lift fillets off the bones

POACHED SALMON WITH LEMON MAYONNAISE
SAUMON POCHÉ DANS UNE MAYONNAISE AU CITRON

Serves 10
*1 whole salmon, about 3 kg (6 lb
10 oz) in weight, cleaned*

For the stock:
500 ml (18 fl oz) white wine
2 litres (3½ pints) water
150 g (5 oz) carrots
100 g (3½ oz) shallots
2 cloves
2 sprigs of thyme
4 sprigs of parsley
white of 1 leek
coarse sea salt
6-8 black peppercorns
chervil, to garnish (optional)

For the lemon mayonnaise:
4 large egg yolks
sea salt
freshly ground white pepper
1 tablespoon Dijon mustard
juice of 1 lemon
500 ml (18 fl oz) olive oil

Prepare the stock ingredients. Wash and trim the carrots, peel and chop the shallots finely, and chop the leek coarsely. Place, with the remaining stock ingredients, in a large saucepan and, without covering, bring to simmering point over a gentle heat. Cook, still uncovered, for a further 30 minutes, then remove from the heat and leave to cool.

Once the stock is quite cooled, strain. Place the salmon in a fish kettle, pour over the stock, cover, and heat until the liquid is simmering, then cook gently for 30 minutes.

Meanwhile, make the mayonnaise. First, ensure that all the ingredients, and the bowl and whisk, are at room temperature. Beat the egg yolks with a pinch of salt, a little freshly ground white pepper, and the mustard, until thick and frothy. Add half the lemon juice and whisk again thoroughly. Add the oil, drop by drop at first, beating well between each addition then, as the mixture thickens, pour in a little more oil each time, but always making sure that the last batch has been thoroughly absorbed before adding the next. When about two-thirds of the oil has been incorporated, whisk in the remaining lemon juice, then gradually beat in the rest of the oil. Taste and adjust the seasoning if necessary. Transfer to a serving bowl or sauceboat and chill until ready to use.

If the fish is cooked before you are ready to serve, it will keep warm in the covered fish kettle, off the heat, for 25-30 minutes. (Alternatively, if you wish to serve it cold, leave to cool, still in the fish kettle to ensure it keeps moist, for 2-3 hours.) Just before serving, transfer the fish carefully on to a clean work surface, cut into 4-5 cm (1½-2 inch) thick steaks, and arrange on a warmed serving platter.

Serve accompanied by the lemon mayonnaise, and garnished with chervil if liked.

Prepare all the stock ingredients, then place in a large saucepan and heat gently, uncovered, until simmering

Pour the cooled and strained stock over the salmon in the fish kettle

To accompany, try an aromatic, fruity Sancerre or Pouilly Fumé,
or a Sauvignon Blanc from New Zealand

Make the mayonnaise in a large bowl, beating the egg yolks first with salt, pepper and mustard, then adding the oil, very gradually at first

Just before serving, cut the fish into 4-5 cm (1½-2 inch) thick steaks, and arrange on a warmed serving platter

15

SALMON AND SPINACH LASAGNE
SAUMON ACCOMPAGNÉ DE LASAGNE AUX ÉPINARDS

Serves 4

For the pasta:
250 g (9 oz) flour
50 g (2 oz) semolina
3 eggs
4 tablespoons olive oil
pinch of sea salt
1 tablespoon water

For the sauce:
1 small shallot, halved
100 ml (3½ fl oz) white wine
3 tablespoons dry vermouth
400 ml (14 fl oz) fish stock (page 151)
225 g (8 oz) butter
5 basil leaves
lemon juice
sea salt

For the filling:
450 g (1 lb) small spinach leaves, well washed
5–6 tomatoes, blanched, skinned, seeded and finely diced
25 g (1 oz) butter, plus extra for frying
5 basil leaves
sea salt
freshly ground black pepper
about 275 g (10 oz) salmon fillet, thinly sliced

For the pasta, mix all the ingredients together either in a food processor, or a large bowl, until the dough leaves the sides clean. Knead until smooth and elastic, then pat into a ball, wrap in cling film and leave to rest for 1 hour.

Pat the dough lightly until flat, then pass several times through the smooth roller of a pasta machine, or roll out by hand on a floured surface until wafer thin. Cut into 10×8 cm (4×3¼ inch) squares, laying out the squares on a floured cloth.

For the sauce, simmer the shallot in the white wine and vermouth until softened, add the fish stock and reduce by two-thirds.

Meanwhile, make the filling. Drain the spinach well. If it is winter spinach, when the leaves can often be thicker and tougher than the new young summer shoots, blanch by pouring boiling water over it, then refresh in cold water and blot dry with kitchen towel. Cook the tomatoes briefly in the butter, add the basil and season lightly. Keep the tomato mixture warm.

Finish the sauce while bringing a large pan of salted water to the boil. Whisk the butter into the reduced fish stock, a piece at a time, until slightly thickened. Add the basil, simmer for a minute or so, then sieve, and return to the pan, off the heat.

Add the lasagne squares to the boiling water and cook for 2–3 minutes until just done but still *al dente*. Meanwhile, quickly melt a small knob of butter and briefly fry the slices of salmon fillet on both sides. Drain the pasta, rinse under warm water to remove excess starch, drain again thoroughly, then, on warm plates, make alternate layers of pasta, tomato, spinach leaves and salmon. Repeat until the lasagne are about 5 cm (2 inches) high, finishing with a square of pasta. Very quickly return the sauce to the heat, add a squeeze of lemon juice, a sprinkling of salt, whisk once, then pour over the lasagne. Serve immediately.

Lay a square of lasagne on a warm plate and cover with tomato

Put a few well-dried spinach leaves on top, sprinkle with pepper if wished

To accompany, try a exhuberant white wine such as an Australian Chardonnay, or a light French red wine such as Anjou or Gamay de Touraine, served slightly chilled

Add a fried slice of salmon, then another square of pasta and some more tomato and spinach

Make further layers of salmon, tomato and spinach, finishing with a square of pasta. Quickly return the sauce to the heat, whisk once, then pour over the lasagne

Catfish Fricassée
FRICASSÉE DE LOUP

Serves 4
1 kg (2 lbs) skinned fillets of catfish
(sometimes sold as rock turbot, or –
erroneously – as rock salmon)
sea salt
freshly ground black pepper
For the vegetable stock:
1 small onion, peeled
1 leek, washed
1 small carrot, scrubbed
1 celery stalk, washed
200 ml (7 fl oz) dry white wine
1 teaspoon tarragon vinegar
1 litre (1¾ pints) water
sea salt
freshly ground black pepper
For the sauce:
175 g (6 oz) butter
1 shallot, peeled and chopped
6 tablespoons dry white wine
2 tablespoons vermouth
500 ml (18 fl oz) fish stock
5–6 tablespoons freshly grated
  horseradish root
sea salt
freshly ground black pepper
To garnish:
2 inner celery stalks, washed
2 carrots, peeled
1 leek, washed
1 tablespoon butter
sea salt
freshly ground black pepper

To make the vegetable stock, chop the vegetables coarsely, place in a large pan with all the other stock ingredients and bring to the boil. Season generously and simmer gently.

For the sauce, melt 2 tablespoons butter, gently fry the shallot to soften, then moisten with the wine and vermouth. Add the fish stock and boil to reduce by two-thirds. Stir about 3 tablespoons of the fresh horseradish into the sauce, and leave to simmer very gently.

Cut the fish fillets into 4×4 cm (1½×1½ inch) pieces. Season with salt and pepper and add to the vegetable stock: poach for about 4–5 minutes, until the fish is firm and opaque.

To make the garnish, cut the vegetables into julienne strips, then soften in 1 tablespoon butter, add a few drops of water, salt and pepper, and cook until just done but still crisp. Add a couple of spoonfuls of the fish poaching liquid and cook for a further 30 seconds, then strain the vegetables, adding their liquid to the sauce. Set the vegetables aside. Reduce the sauce a little more until smooth and glossy then stir in the julienne strips.

Drain the fish pieces from the stock, and add to the sauce. Steep briefly, remove, and keep warm. Dice the remaining butter, then beat into the sauce, a knob at a time, and adjust the seasoning.

Serve the fish with the sauce poured over, scattering the remaining strips of horseradish on top.

Put the seasoned fillets of fish into boiling stock, reduce the heat to a simmer

Gently fry the vegetables for the garnish to soften. Add a little of the fish poaching liquid

To accompany, try a fresh white wine such as Muscadet de Sèvre-et-Maine sur lie *or Alsace Sylvaner*

Cook briefly, then pour off the liquid and add to the sauce

Reduce the sauce slightly, add the vegetable strips and drained catfish pieces. Steep briefly, then remove the fish and stir the butter into the sauce

EELS IN ASPIC WITH CHICK PEAS
ASPIC D'ANGUILLES ACCOMPAGNÉ DE POIS CHICHES

Serves 8 *[a terrine 25 × 8 cm
(10 × 3¼ inches) and 8 cm (3¼
inches) deep]*
*7 gelatine leaves, or 15 g (½ oz)
powdered gelatine*
*300 g (11 oz) chick peas, soaked
overnight*
250 g (9 oz) French beans, trimmed
140 ml (4½ fl oz) white wine
250 g (9 oz) tiny button mushrooms
*800 g (1¾ lbs) smoked eel, skinned
and filleted (skin and bones reserved)*
4 egg whites
lemon juice
*750 ml (27 fl oz) fish stock (page
151)*
1 teaspoon dry vermouth
sea salt

For the sauce:
1 egg yolk
½ teaspoon mustard
2 tablespoons sherry vinegar
2 tablespoons white wine vinegar
sea salt
freshly ground black pepper
125 ml (4 fl oz) vegetable oil
*2 tablespoons reduced brown veal
stock (page 150)*
juice of ¼ lemon
½ apple, peeled and finely diced
*1 tablespoon freshly grated
horseradish*
1 tablespoon apple juice

Put the gelatine in a small bowl with a little water and leave to soften and swell.

Drain the chick peas, then put to simmer in fresh water, salted, for 1 hour until soft but not mushy. Blanch the beans in boiling salted water for 2–3 minutes, then refresh in cold water.

Reserve 1 tablespoon of the white wine, bring the rest to the boil, then put the mushrooms to steam over the wine for 2–3 minutes. Keep aside, together with the drained chick peas and the beans. Chop the eel fillets into lengths which will fit the terrine.

To make the aspic, whisk the egg whites with lemon juice until frothy, then stir into the fish stock in a large wide pan. Add the eel skin and bones and bring to the boil, then boil to reduce by one-third – the egg white will have formed a crust on top drawing up into it all the impurities. Remove from the heat, push the white aside gently and stir in the drained gelatine until dissolved, disturbing the whites as little as possible.

Gently pour the stock through a fine muslin – it should be crystal clear. Leave to cool, then stir in the remaining white wine, the vermouth and a little salt. Pour some of the syrupy aspic into the terrine to a depth of 0.5 cm (about ¼ inch) and put to set in the refrigerator.

If necessary, slightly heat the remaining aspic until just liquid, dip in the beans then make a layer of beans on the set aspic in the terrine. Pour over a little aspic just to cover, then chill to set. Make layers of eel, mushrooms and chick peas in the same way, finishing with a layer of eel, and topping with the remaining aspic. Chill for 2 hours.

For the sauce, beat the egg yolk, mustard and vinegars together with a good seasoning of salt and pepper, then add the oil gradually, stirring constantly. Once you have a good emulsion, add the veal stock and lemon juice, then stir in the apple, horseradish and apple juice. Whisk briskly and adjust the seasoning if necessary.

To serve, dip the terrine into very hot water, quickly running a sharp knife round the sides, then turn out on to a plate. Cut into eight slices and serve on individual plates with a little sauce on each.

Dissolve the drained gelatine in the hot fish stock, off the stove

Gently strain the stock through a fine muslin

To accompany, try a medium-dry white wine, such as Vouvray or
Coteaux du Layon demi sec

Make a layer of aspic in the terrine and, once set, arrange some beans on top, previously dipped in the liquid aspic, then cover with a little more aspic

Make similar layers with the remaining ingredients, topping with the rest of the liquid aspic. Chill for 2 hours to set

RED MULLET WITH A BASIL DRESSING
ROUGET AVEC ASSAISONNEMENT AU BASILIC

Serves 4

4 red mullet, each weighing 400 g
 (14 oz), scaled and cleaned
sea salt
freshly ground black pepper
3 tablespoons olive oil

For the dressing:

sea salt
freshly ground black pepper
2 tablespoons lemon juice
2 tablespoons chopped basil leaves
6 tablespoons olive oil

To garnish:

few curly lettuce leaves, washed
few leaves of lamb's lettuce, washed

Cut off the fish heads at an angle, slipping the knife blade under the fins to remove them too. Then make an incision along the backbone and slide the knife between the flesh and bone, gently easing the fillets off the bone. Or ask your fishmonger to fillet the fish.

Pat the fillets dry with kitchen towel, and remove the small side bones using a pair of tweezers. Lightly season the fish with salt and pepper. Heat the olive oil in a pan (non-stick if possible), add the fillets, skin side down, and fry gently without browning. Turn and cook for a further 2–3 minutes. Remove the fillets from the pan and place on kitchen towel to absorb any excess fat.

For the basil dressing, stir a little salt and pepper into the lemon juice, then mix in the basil leaves and olive oil. Turn the fillets in the basil dressing several times to coat thoroughly – but work quickly as the fish should still be warm when served.

On each of four plates arrange a few leaves of curly lettuce and two fillets. Garnish with the lamb's lettuce, then sprinkle on the remaining basil dressing.

Cut off the heads at an angle and fillet the fish

Using tweezers pull out all the small side bones

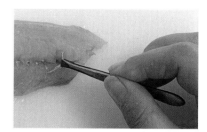

*To accompany, try a bright rosé wine such as Côtes de Provence rosé,
or a chilled Fino sherry*

Fry the seasoned fillets, skin side first,
then turn carefully

Lay the fried fillets on kitchen towel to
drain excess fat, then coat with the basil
dressing

STUFFED TURBOT WITH TARRAGON SAUCE
TURBOT FARCI SAUCE À L'ESTRAGON

Serves 4

*1 chicken turbot, about 1.2 kg (2³⁄4
  lbs), cleaned and the backbone
  removed from the dark-skinned side*
sea salt
freshly ground black pepper
15 g (¹⁄2 oz) butter
*250 ml (9 fl oz) fish stock (page
  151)*

For the stuffing:

*40 g (1¹⁄2 oz) finely diced vegetables,
  a mixture of celery, leek, carrot*
1 teaspoon butter
125 g (4 oz) pike fillets, chilled
salt and pepper
freshly grated nutmeg
1 egg, chilled
125 ml (4 fl oz) double cream, chilled
3 tablespoons whipping cream

For the sauce:

1 teaspoon tarragon vinegar
8 tarragon leaves, chopped
salt and pepper
100 ml (3¹⁄2 fl oz) white wine
1 tablespoon dry champagne
2 tablespoons dry vermouth
400 ml (14 fl oz) fish stock
200 ml (7 fl oz) double cream
25 g (1 oz) butter

To garnish:

2 tomatoes, skinned and diced
1 tablespoon butter
a few basil leaves, chopped

To make the stuffing, gently fry the diced vegetables in butter until soft but not browned, leave to cool, then chill.

Cut the filleted pike into small pieces, season with salt, pepper and nutmeg and purée in a food processor or blender. Add the chilled egg, blend again, then gradually add the double cream, blending between each addition. Adjust the seasoning, then push the purée through a fine sieve, and chill for 30 minutes.

Season the inside of the turbot with salt and pepper. Mix the chilled diced vegetables with the pike purée, and add the whipping cream. Stuff the turbot with the mixture and place in a buttered, ovenproof dish. Pour over the fish stock and cook in the oven, preheated to 200°C/400°F/gas 6 for approximately 20 minutes.

To make the sauce, reduce the tarragon vinegar with the chopped tarragon, until the liquid is completely evaporated. Add salt and pepper, the wine, champagne, vermouth and fish stock, and boil until reduced by three-quarters, to leave a scant 150 ml (¼ pint) of liquid. Stir in the double cream and simmer the sauce for about 10 minutes, until well thickened.

For the garnish, gently fry the tomatoes in a little butter, then stir in the chopped basil.

Place the cooked turbot carefully on a large, hot plate: strain the cooking liquor and whisk into the sauce, then beat the remaining 25 g (1 oz) butter into the sauce, a small piece at a time, until smooth and glossy. Pass the sauce through a fine sieve.

Skin the turbot, spoon the tomato and basil mixture over the filling, then remove the fish fins, tail and head. Divide the fish into portions, and serve on a bed of sauce.

Carefully remove the skin from the cooked turbot

Arrange the tomato and basil mixture on top of the stuffing

*To accompany, try a fine white wine from Burgundy, such as a
Meursault or Chablis Premier Cru, or a still Coteaux Champenois*

Using two tablespoons remove the fins,
the bony edges and the tail

Carefully remove the head, and divide
the stuffed turbot into four portions

FILLETS OF PLAICE IN HERB SAUCE
FILETS DE CARRELET SAUCE AUX FINES HERBES

Serves 4

2 medium-sized plaice, cleaned
sea salt
2–3 tablespoons sunflower or peanut
* oil*

For the herb sauce:

500 ml (18 fl oz) dry white wine
5 tablespoons dry vermouth
3 shallots, finely chopped
250 ml (9 fl oz) fish stock (page
* 151)*
75 g (3 oz) butter, chilled and diced
lemon juice
sea salt
2 small tomatoes, blanched, skinned
* and seeded*
1 tablespoon butter
1 tablespoon finely chopped chervil
1 tablespoon finely chopped tarragon
½ teaspoon finely chopped basil
2 tablespoons whipping cream

To make the herb sauce, bring the wine, vermouth and shallots to the boil. Add the fish stock and reduce the liquid by half.

With a pair of kitchen scissors, cut off the fish heads, following the natural curve. Then make an incision in the plaice on the dark-skinned side through to the centre backbone. Slip the knife blade between the bones and the flesh working towards the side fins to separate one fillet. Detach the remaining fillets the same way.

Lay the fillets on a firm surface, skin side down, and loosen the skin slightly at the tail end. Hold the skin firmly, insert a sharp knife between the skin and the fillet and draw the knife forward, easing the flesh off the skin. Cut away the fine fin bones along the edge of each fillet.

Season the fish lightly with salt and fry gently on both sides in hot oil. Drain on kitchen towel to absorb excess fat, then keep warm.

Stir the chilled butter into the sauce, a knob at a time, whisking well before the next addition. Briefly bring the sauce to the boil, then pass through a fine sieve, season with a dash of lemon juice and salt, and mix thoroughly. Finely dice the tomatoes and fry gently in a tablespoon of just sizzling butter. Add to the sauce together with the herbs and cream, again whisking well.

Pour some sauce on to individual plates, place two fillets on top and serve immediately.

Cut through the dark-skinned side of the plaice to the centre backbone

Slide the knife blade between the flesh and bones to separate into fillets

*To accompany, try a white wine from the Riesling grape, such as
Alsace Riesling or a Riesling Rabinett from the Rheingau*

To skin, use a very sharp knife, start at
the tail end and slide it gently but firmly
between the skin and fillet. A little salt
on the fingers of the hand holding the
skin helps grip it more easily

Trim away the fine fin bones down the
side of each fillet

POACHED HADDOCK WITH MUSTARD BUTTER

HADDOCK POCHÉ AU BEURRE À LA MOUTARDE

Serves 4

1 small haddock, about 2 kg
(4½ lbs), scaled and cleaned
4.5 litres (8 pints) water
sea salt
1 bay leaf
½ onion, coarsely chopped
10 peppercorns
250 ml (9 fl oz) tarragon vinegar
freshly ground black pepper

For the mustard butter:

1 red pepper, washed, halved, then
* pith and seeds removed*
125 g (4 oz) butter
2 teaspoons green peppercorn mustard
3 teaspoons finely chopped chervil
lemon juice
sea salt

Clean the haddock in cold running water and dry on kitchen towel. Insert a large needle threaded with kitchen cotton into the head of the fish below the eyes. Draw the cotton through, put the tail of the fish into its mouth and pass one end of the thread around the tail. Tie the ends of the thread together in a knot and cut off the ends.

In a very large oval pan or flameproof casserole, bring the water to the boil with salt, the bay leaf, onion, peppercorns and tarragon vinegar. Place the haddock on a large holed trivet (or a rack), then lower gently into the boiling stock and cook, covered, for 15–20 minutes over a moderate heat.

To make the mustard butter, finely dice the pepper halves. Melt the butter in a pan until foaming and lightly browned, meanwhile mixing the mustard with the chervil and lemon juice. Add the diced pepper to the pan, season lightly with salt, then gradually stir in the mustard and lemon mixture.

Lift the fish out of the stock and snip off the cotton. With a sharp knife, carefully make an incision along the backbone of the fish and peel away the skin from top to bottom. Using a tablespoon, lift portion-sized pieces of fish off the bones, serve on the mustard butter and season with black pepper.

NOTE: If you are unable to obtain a whole haddock, you could use 1 kg (2 lbs) haddock fillet instead and poach for 10–12 minutes.

Insert a large needle threaded with kitchen cotton through the jaws of the fish, and draw the cotton through

Place the tail of the fish in its mouth, wind one end of the thread around the outside, then tie with a knot

*To accompany, try a spicy white wine such as Gewürztraminer from
Alsace or Traminer from Alto Adige*

Place the haddock on a large holed
trivet and lower into the stock

After poaching, remove and drain.
Make an incision along the backbone
and carefully remove the skin from the
top downwards

Salted Herrings in Aspic with Herb Sauce

ASPIC DE HARENGS SALÉS SAUCE AUX FINES HERBES

Serves 6

500 ml (18 fl oz) dry white wine

250 ml (9 fl oz) water

2 tablespoons vinegar

1 bouquet garni

1 onion, unpeeled

1 carrot, scrubbed

1 leek, washed and split down the
  middle

1 celery stick, washed

1 bay leaf

2 cloves

2 juniper berries

5 peppercorns

sugar

sea salt

14 leaves of gelatine, or 25 g (1 oz)
  powdered gelatine

4 egg whites

3 tablespoons beetroot juice

8 salted herring fillets

2 large gherkins

2–3 pickled baby beetroots

For the sauce:

250 ml (9 fl oz) crème fraîche

250 ml (9 fl oz) milk

2 tablespoons orange juice

sea salt

sugar

freshly ground black pepper

1 small bunch each of dill, chervil,
  chives, parsley and mustard cress,
  finely chopped

Put the wine, water, vinegar and bouquet garni in a large pan and bring to the boil. Wipe the onion clean, then pin the bay leaf to the onion with the cloves. Add to the court bouillon with the carrot, leek and celery, juniper berries, peppercorns, a pinch of sugar and a little salt: simmer for 30 minutes.

Then pour through a fine sieve and leave to cool. Soften the gelatine in a small bowl of cold water. Beat the egg whites very lightly, then pour into a saucepan. Add the court bouillon, whisk briskly and slowly bring to the boil, whisking continuously. Simmer for 5 minutes, then pass through a fine muslin into a scrupulously clean bowl. The egg white and all impurities will be strained out to leave a crystal-clear soup. Squeeze the gelatine leaves of excess moisture and stir into the hot court bouillon to dissolve. Powdered gelatine will probably have absorbed all the liquid and will merely need to be stirred thoroughly into the bouillon. Then add the beetroot juice, again mixing well.

Cool quickly by setting the bowl in a larger bowl full of ice cubes, but do not allow to set. Keep an eye on it, stirring occasionally. Cut the herring fillets into small pieces, about 3 cm (1¼ inches). Halve the gherkins lengthwise, discard the seeds and dice finely, then dice the beetroot. Pour the thickened but still liquid jelly into individual moulds to a depth of 0.5 cm (¼ inch), and chill to set.

Then cover with alternate layers of the diced vegetables and pieces of herring, topping up with the remaining jelly. Chill in the refrigerator for 6 hours.

To make the herb sauce, beat all ingredients together until thick and frothy, test for seasoning, adjusting if necessary. If wished, purée in a blender for a greener sauce.

Divide the sauce between six plates. Briefly dip the jelly moulds in hot water, loosen the edge of the jellies with a knife, turn out and serve on top of the sauce.

Arrange alternate layers of diced vegetables and herring pieces in the prepared moulds

Cover with the cool but still liquid jelly. Chill in the refrigerator to set

To accompany, try a chilled Fino sherry, or a strong,
dry Normandy cider

Before turning out, dip the moulds in hot water

With a knife, carefully release the edge of the jelly from the mould and turn out. Serve on the herb sauce

ICED PEPPER SOUP WITH LANGOUSTINES
SOUPE DE POIVRONS GLACÉE AUX LANGOUSTINES

Serves 4
2–3 red peppers, to give 175 ml (6 fl oz) juice
1 small cucumber, to give 150 ml (¼ pint) juice
250 g (9 oz) tomatoes, to give 200 ml (7 fl oz) juice
2 egg yolks
100 ml (3½ fl oz) wheatgerm oil (available from health shops; once opened, keep in the refrigerator, well sealed, and use as quickly as possible since it rapidly deteriorates)
5 tablespoons olive oil
sea salt
freshly ground black pepper
red wine vinegar
1 small garlic clove, peeled
To garnish:
12 fresh langoustines
sea salt
freshly ground white pepper

The moisture content of vegetables varies immensely depending on the freshness, so it is difficult to give precise quantities. Err on the side of generosity and any left-over juice will give you a delicious drink.

Peel, halve and core the peppers. Put the peppers into a blender with a little water, and blend to a purée. Pour into a bowl and rinse out the blender. Peel and core the cucumber, cut into pieces and purée. Again, rinse the blender. Wash, quarter and purée the tomatoes, then sieve to remove skin and seeds. For a particularly fine soup, strain the other purées too, through a muslin or fine sieve.

Beat the egg yolks with the two oils, adding them little by little at first, then in a slow trickle to make a mayonnaise. Mix together with the vegetable juices: season with salt, pepper and a splash of red wine vinegar. Crush the garlic and stir into the soup. Or, for a very mild flavour of garlic, pierce the clove with a fork and draw through the soup several times. Put in the refrigerator to chill thoroughly.

For the garnish, pull off and discard the heads of the langoustines. Peel off the tail shell and carefully extract the flesh in one piece. Then scrape out the intestines – the thin black thread running through the centre of the tail. Sometimes this is quite visible but you may have to make a slight incision along the centre of the back of the tail before it can be pulled out.

Lightly season the langoustines, put into a saucepan with a little water, and cook, covered, for 2–3 minutes, until the flesh is pink and firm. Serve the soup, ice cold, in chilled dishes, with three langoustines placed in the centre of each dish to garnish.

Langoustines, also known as Norway lobsters, or Dublin Bay prawns, can be bought fresh or frozen, with or without their heads, though only the tails are eaten. If you buy whole langoustines pull off and discard the head

Split and peel off the tail shell. Take hold of the tail flesh . . .

*To accompany, try a Côtes de Provence rosé,
or a Portuguese Vinho Verde*

. . . and withdraw it carefully from the shell, to keep in one piece

Remove the bitter intestines, a thin black thread running through the centre of the tail. If necessary, cut gently through the topside of the tail to the middle until the intestines are visible, then scrape out

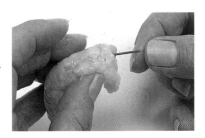

LOBSTER AND FRESH PEA SOUP
SOUPE DE HOMARD ET DE PETIS POIS FRAIS

Serves 4
2 small live lobsters, each weighing 400 g (14 oz), boiled for approximately 10 minutes in salted water

75 g (3 oz) shallots, chopped

150 g (5 oz) butter

450 g (1 lb) fresh peas, shelled

700 ml−1 litre (1¼−1¾ pints) chicken stock (page 149)

sea salt

freshly ground black pepper

sugar

5 tablespoons whipping cream

To garnish:
75 g (3 oz) streaky bacon, finely diced

15 g (½ oz) butter

12 spring onions, trimmed to leave about 5 cm (2 inches) above the bulb

10 lettuce heart leaves, finely shredded

Leave the lobsters to cool in their boiling liquid, and once cool enough to handle, separate the head and claws from the tail by first inserting a knife tip to loosen the joint, then rotate and pull apart. Turn the head over on to the shell side and split open with a heavy knife or cleaver. Remove the stomach sac (near the top of the head) and discard, then scoop out the greeny-beige coloured liver (the tomally) with a spoon, and set aside. Cut through the soft shell on the belly side of the tail with a pair of kitchen scissors and extract the flesh in one piece. Remove the intestines (a thin black vein which runs down the back of the tail).

Break off the claws from the head, and crack the shell with a heavy-bladed knife, or lobster crackers.

Extract the flesh, including the plastic-like sheet of cartilage which should be discarded. Try to keep the flesh from the claw tip intact. Using a lobster pick, or skewer, remove the flesh from the legs and pincer joints and reserve.

Sweat the shallots in 50 g (2 oz) butter, until soft but not coloured. Add the peas and 700 ml (1¼ pints) chicken stock, season lightly with salt and pepper and simmer for approximately 15 minutes, adding the reserved tomally after 10 minutes.

Purée the soup in a blender, pass through a fine sieve, return to the saucepan, and adjust the seasoning adding extra salt and pepper to taste plus a pinch of sugar. If it seems too thick, add some more chicken stock.

For the garnish, gently fry the bacon in a little butter, add the spring onions and shredded lettuce, and cook over a low heat for a further 2−3 minutes. Set aside.

Heat the soup, gradually whisking in the remaining butter and the cream. Cut the lobster tails into small rounds, and arrange with the leg and joint flesh in individual soup plates. Divide the fried bacon/spring onion garnish between the bowls, then pour over the soup. Garnish each serving with a claw tip.

Using a knife, insert point of blade to loosen the tail of the lobster from the head

Rotate and pull off the head and claws

To accompany, try a fresh white wine such as Muscadet de Sèvre-et-Maine sur lie, *or a fine, dry style of Madeira, such as Extra Reserve Sercial or Verdelho*

Using a pair of kitchen scissors, snip through the soft shell on the belly side of the tail

Carefully remove the flesh from the shell. Break off the claws and thin leg joints from the head and pick out the flesh, being careful to keep the claw tip intact

SCALLOPS IN SORREL SAUCE
COQUILLES SAINT-JACQUES SAUCE À L'OSEILLE

Serves 4
12–16 fresh medium-sized scallops
*   with corals, or frozen scallop meat*
*   with corals*
sea salt
freshly ground black pepper
25 g (1 oz) butter
For the sauce:
25 g (1 oz) butter
1 shallot, chopped
4 tablespoons white wine
4 tablespoons dry vermouth
100 ml (3½ fl oz) fish stock (page
*   151)*
5 tablespoons double cream
65 g (2½ oz) butter, chilled and
*   diced*
sea salt
freshly ground black pepper
25 g (1 oz) sorrel leaves, washed,
*   trimmed and finely chopped*

Remove fresh scallops from their shells, rinse and soak the meat, including the orange roe, for 1 hour in cold water. Allow frozen scallops to thaw.

For the sauce, melt the butter, add the shallot and fry gently to soften. Moisten with the white wine and vermouth, add the fish stock and cream, raise the heat and boil the sauce vigorously.

Drain the scallop meat, cut out and discard any black bits and the greyish gristle around each white cushion. Cut the scallops in half vertically to leave one half with, and the other without, the roe. Season with salt and pepper. Melt the butter in a pan and lightly fry the scallops on each side without browning. Drain on kitchen towel to absorb excess fat.

Beat the butter, a piece at a time, into the sauce to thicken and make glossy. Adjust the seasoning if necessary, and stir in the finely chopped sorrel leaves. Arrange the scallops on individual plates, and spoon over the sauce.

The orange tongue, in fact the roe, is called the coral, and regarded as a delicacy

Briefly fry the halved, seasoned scallops in moderately hot butter

*To accompany, try a fresh, dry white Loire wine, such as Quincy or
Pouilly Fumé*

For the sauce, gently fry the shallots in hot butter. Moisten with the wine and vermouth

Pour on the fish stock and cream, bring to the boil, then bind the sauce with chilled, diced butter. Adjust the seasoning, then stir in the sorrel leaves

37

MUSSELS IN CURRY SAUCE
MOULES SAUCE AU CURRY

Serves 4

56 fresh mussels (approximately 1–
1.1 kg/2–2½ pints)

For the broth:

200 ml (7 fl oz) Riesling
150 ml (¼ pint) water
1 small shallot, finely chopped
1 garlic clove, finely chopped
1 sprig of thyme

For the sauce:

1–2 teaspoons curry powder
juice of ½ lemon
200 ml (7 fl oz) double cream
1 small shallot, chopped
5 tablespoons dry white wine
3 tablespoons dry vermouth
freshly ground black pepper
8–12 fresh lychees
20 g (scant 1 oz) butter, flaked
2 tablespoons whipping cream, lightly
whipped

To garnish:

1 red pepper, halved, seeds and pith
removed
knob of butter
whipped cream

Scrub the mussels thoroughly under cold running water and remove the beards – they'll need quite a sharp tug. Discard any mussels that don't close when sharply tapped – they are dead. Place the broth ingredients in a large pan, bring to the boil and throw in the mussels (do in two batches if necessary, the layer should not be too deep).

Cover and leave to cook for 4–5 minutes, then remove the mussels, discarding any that have not opened – they too are dead. Strain the broth through a muslin to catch any sand or grit, and keep aside. Shell the mussels, discarding the shells.

Return the broth to a clean pan, add the curry powder, 1 teaspoon at first, and the lemon juice and bring to the boil. Add the double cream, shallot, wine, vermouth and a good sprinkling of pepper then boil to reduce by half. Taste after about 5 minutes and add more curry powder if you think it needs it, but the flavour should be subtle rather than overpowering. Meanwhile, peel the lychees, split down one side and remove the stones.

Place the pepper for the garnish on a baking sheet and put in the oven, preheated to 220°C/425°F/gas 7, for 10–15 minutes. Transfer to a bowl of iced water and, when cool, rub off the skin, then slice the pepper finely and keep aside.

Once the sauce is reduced, whisk quickly, then stir in the butter, a few flakes at a time. Add the mussels and lychees to warm through. Meanwhile, in another pan, quickly toss the pepper strips in a small knob of butter, then season lightly. Add the whipped cream to the mussels, adjust the seasoning if necessary, then pile into warm soup plates and garnish with the red pepper and a spoonful or so of whipped cream.

Put the scrubbed, debearded mussels into the boiling broth

Cover and simmer for 4–5 minutes

To accompany, try a broad, rich white wine such as Hermitage or a Californian Chardonnay

Drain the mussels, and strain the broth

Using a knife, remove the mussels from the shells

MEAT

SEVERAL CHARACTERISTICS MARK THE REALM of meat cookery in the French kitchen. First, there is the way the actual butchering of the meat is carried out, especially in the case of beef, and even more so in the case of veal. Then there is the distinct penchant the French have for rarity in their meat (with the obvious exception of pork), not shared as a whole by the English-speaking races. And third, they have a love of veal, a meat about which some are curiously ambivalent. Perhaps this is an unconscious echo of our ancestors' Anglo-Saxon resentment toward the Normans who prized veal highly; the native people, however, counted their wealth in cattle and did not care to see their riches being diminished at so early an age. The battery farming of recent times, together with the youth of the animals at death, merely reinforced much of the prejudice against this meat. But trends are changing, and it should not be difficult today to find freely reared veal. And, though 'the best veal comes from sucking calves ... it is important that they are not too young. They should be between eight and ten months old. These animals have particularly tender yet firm flesh'.

Bocuse also shares his countrymen's love of the cheaper cuts of meat. 'In my view, the best parts of the calf are the head and offal. I would take a calf's head with vinaigrette every time in preference to any fillet. And my favourite dish, the *pot-au-feu*, should always include a veal shank, just as much as an oxtail.' His treatment of these cuts clearly reveals his respect for them: the pieces of oxtail carefully boned out and stuffed, the calf's head served with slices of tongue, the stuffed pig's trotter simply presented – but with a superb sauce.

In the restaurant, Bocuse offers as the *amuse gueule* a tasting of Cervelas, a wonderful Lyonnais sausage – but one more usually to be found among the charcuterie of much humbler establishment. Proud of his native town ('Paris is a suburb of Lyons'), he lists other local *saucissons* on his menu, too. And when cooking his favourite *pot-au-feu* at home, the dish will include not only the veal shank, and oxtail, but also beef shank and skirt, plus a piece of lean steak, neck of lamb and a chicken – with slices of truffle placed under the skin. A regal pot indeed.

Marriages of the simple to the exoctic, the expensive ingredient to the cheap, abound in Bocuse's cooking. Pork fillet is accompanied not by truffles, but a mushroom risotto, and a young loin is partnered with cabbage, a vegetable not usually associated with *haute cuisine*. But such combinations are the very essence of traditional country cooking – a tradition in which Bocuse delights.

He respects, too, the age-old adherence to the seasons: 'Spring

lamb is undoubtedly the best, but it is only available for a short period of time. But then come the lambs from the Alpine mountain pastures which have an excellent flavour thanks to the many herbs that they eat, and above all the *pré-sale* lambs. They include those from the salt meadows of the French coast.' Such creatures need but the simplest of treatments. Bocuse roasts his best end of neck on the spit; the saddle, even more delicately treated, has a gentle poaching to keep it moist and lightly pink inside. For the French have always preferred their lamb rosy, if not rare. A liking for well-done meat is a puzzling to them as partnering it with mint sauce. The young Marcel Boulestin, returning home from his first trip to England, was asked in amazement by his father, 'Do you mean to say that they really eat mint with lamb?' Boulestin's assurance that indeed it was so, produced an incredulous shake of the head: 'What a funny country!' Boulestin, in fact, was a rarity among his compatriots in liking mint sauce, and he went to endless lengths to find the right variety of the herb, unaware until many years later that the family was so large that the species he sought was unavailable in France....

With beef too, there are differences. Rarity is definitely the norm for steaks; rump, which we normally would serve as a steak, is often used for gently cooked, melt-in-the-mouth casseroles; while fillet will as often be poached as grilled or roasted. Irrespective of the method of cooking, or 'where it comes from, beef must be an attractive red colour. It must be marbled with fat and properly matured, i.e. it must be hung for a sufficient length of time'.

The beef in Bocuse's kitchen comes from the distinctively cream-coloured Charolais, native to neighbouring Mâcon. Slaughtered at six rather than the normal five years, it is nevertheless extraordinarily tender, though many (in France, as well as Britain) deem the Scottish Angus to be equally fine.

The species of pig, on the other hand, is less important than its diet. The Romans knew this and fed their pigs chestnuts to sweeten and simultaneously fatten them. For 'the pig is an omnivorous animal, and its flesh will easily take on the flavour of what it eats. What the animal is fed with is therefore very important from the point of view of its flavour. Ideally it should be potatoes and lots of green vegetables. And just as the pig eats everything, so it is totally edible for man – from head to foot, the pig is a total delight'.

From time immemorial, the pig has probably been one of man's most important providers. Every smallholder had his own animal: indeed even townsfolk kept pigs. Paris, London, New York and Naples all knew pigs on their streets – New York only banishing them at the end of the last century, the Neapolitans at the beginning of this. Treasured and fattened up for the ritual autumn slaughter, the pig gave bountifully. Black puddings, brawns, the innards for pies, sausages for boiling or curing, caul for larding, fat for cooking, trotters for jelly, hams for the winter. The pig was truly a feast on its own.

RUMP STEAKS BOCUSE
ROMSTECKS BOCUSE

Serves 4

4 – 5 tablespoons clarified butter (see Note), plus extra for frying

450 g (1 lb) white onions, finely chopped

sea salt

freshly ground black pepper

4 rump steaks, about 125 g (4 oz) each in weight, trimmed of fat

4 egg yolks

1 – 2 teaspoons green pepper mustard

2 tablespoons flour

125 ml (4 fl oz) brown veal stock (page 150)

Melt 4 tablespoons butter and, when just sizzling, add the onions and fry until nicely golden, adding more butter if necessary. Season lightly with salt and pepper, then drain in a sieve, and spread on kitchen towel to absorb excess fat.

Place the steaks between two pieces of cling film and gently flatten with a meat bat. Season with salt and pepper on one side, then turn over. Mix the egg yolks with the mustard, season lightly, and brush the steaks liberally with the mixture. Top each steak with some onion, pressing down well with the back of a spoon and covering right to the edges. Sprinkle over a little flour.

Melt a small knob of clarified butter in a large frying pan and fry the steaks, onion-side down, for about 2 minutes. Turn over carefully, season and fry for a further 2 minutes.

Transfer, onion-side up, to warm plates, add the veal stock to the pan and bubble briefly to lightly glaze. Serve the steaks with a little gravy and sauté potatoes.

NOTE: Clarified butter is much used for frying when high temperatures are required as it burns less easily than butter. To make, simply start off with twice the required amount (or make in quantity – it will keep, chilled, for several weeks), and gently melt in a pan. As soon as it is competely melted, pour carefully through a muslin making sure all the white froth (which contains the impurities that cause butter to burn) is caught in the muslin. If a little does get through, remove with a spoon – the resulting liquid should be golden and crystal clear.

Salt and pepper the steaks, then brush with the egg yolk and mustard mixture

Cover with a layer of cooked onion, pressing it down well with a spoon

*To accompany, try a generous, Merlot-based Bordeaux from
Saint-Émilion or Pomerol*

Sprinkle lightly with flour

Fry the steaks, onion-side down, in
butter, turn over, season and fry the
other side

POACHED FILLET OF BEEF
FILET DE BOEUF POCHÉ

Serves 4

*500 ml (18 fl oz) brown veal stock
(page 150)*

*12 spring onions, trimmed to leave
about 5 cm (2 inches) dark green
stalk*

*5 medium-sized carrots, cut in half
lengthways then chopped into 2.5
cm (1 inch) pieces*

*4 small courgettes, trimmed, then cut
in half lengthways and chopped into
2.5 cm (1 inch) pieces*

*2 medium-sized leeks, sliced into 0.5
cm (¼ inch) rings*

12 broccoli florets

450 g (1 lb) fillet of beef

For the dressing:

3 tablespoons red wine vinegar

3 tablespoons water

5 tablespoons olive oil

sea salt

freshly ground black pepper

*2 teaspoons finely chopped herbs
(oregano, chervil, chives and parsley)*

Bring the stock to the boil in a wide, shallow pan, add the spring onions, carrots, courgettes and leeks and simmer for 2 minutes, then add the broccoli and simmer for a further 5–6 minutes.

Meanwhile, slice the beef very finely, using either a very sharp knife or the smooth blade of a slicing machine.

For the dressing, mix all the ingredients together until well emulsified, adjust the seasoning, if necessary, and reserve.

Lift the vegetables out of the stock with a slotted spoon, drain well and keep warm.

With the stock at the merest simmer, drop in the meat, leave it for barely a minute – the beef should be beautifully pink and absorb some of the juices – then quickly remove and arrange on four warmed plates. Surround with the vegetables, a little stock poured over them, then lightly salt and pepper the meat, whisk the dressing and pour over the fillet.

Simmer the vegetables in the stock for 7–8 minutes, adding the broccoli after 2 minutes

Drain the vegetables, cover and keep hot

*To accompany, try a lively Loire red from Chinon or Bourgueil, or a
fine Médoc, such as Margaux or Saint-Julien*

Put the slices of fillet into the just
simmering stock

Let them steep briefly – the meat
should be just lightly poached, pink and
succulent

Braised Beef and Vegetables
BOEUF BRAISÉ AUX LÉGUMES

Serves 4

4 slices rump steak or topside, about
* 175 g (6 oz) each*
freshly ground black pepper
sea salt
1 tablespoon clarified butter (page
* 42)*
250 g (9 oz) onions, coarsely chopped
75 g (3 oz) carrots, scraped, then
* finely diced*
75 g (3 oz) Hamburg parsley or
* celeriac, sliced*
½ teaspoon mild paprika
1 sprig of marjoram, leaves stripped
* off the stalk*
1 sprig of parsley, stalk cut off
grated zest of ½ lemon (lemon well
* washed first)*
400 ml (14 fl oz) veal stock (page
* 150)*
125 ml (4 fl oz) crème fraîche
50 g (2 oz) butter, chilled and flaked
lemon juice (optional)
1 tablespoon capers, chopped

For the garnish:

75 g (3 oz) carrots, washed
75 g (3 oz) leeks, pale green part
* only, washed*
75 g (3 oz) celery, washed
75 g (3 oz) Hamburg parsley or
* celeriac, washed*
sea salt

Place the meat between two layers of cling film and flatten with a meat bat. Lightly season with pepper and salt. Melt the butter, add the meat and quickly sear on both sides, remove from the pan and set aside.

Add the onions to the pan and fry until softened but not coloured, then add the carrots and Hamburg parsley or celeriac and fry for a minute or so. Transfer the vegetables to a casserole, add the paprika, marjoram, parsley and lemon zest, then place the meat on the bed of vegetables. Pour in the juices that have seeped out of the beef, then add the veal stock. Cover and cook in the oven, preheated to 200°C/400°F/gas 6, for about 1 hour.

For the garnish, cut the vegetables into julienne strips about 5 cm (2 inches) long and blanch in salted boiling water for 5 minutes, then drain well and reserve.

Remove the beef from the casserole with a slotted spoon and keep warm on a plate over hot water. Purée the gravy in a blender (or mash the vegetables as finely as possible with a potato masher), then strain through a fine sieve into a pan. Add the crème fraîche, stirring well to blend in, then reduce the sauce slightly.

Whisk in the butter, a few flakes at a time, until the sauce is smooth and glossy then adjust the seasoning, if necessary, adding a squeeze of lemon juice to sharpen lightly if wished. Add the julienne vegetables and capers and heat through, then serve the beef with the gravy poured over, the vegetables on top. Dumplings or tagliatelle make excellent accompaniments.

Sear the beef on both sides then remove from the pan

Add the onions and fry, then add the carrots and Hamburg parsley or celeriac and cook a little longer before seasoning

To accompany, try a red wine from the southern Rhône such as
Châteauneuf-du-Pape or Lirac

Place the meat on a bed of vegetables
and pour in the juices

Add the stock, cover and cook in the
oven, preheated to 200°C/400°F/gas 6,
for 1 hour

STUFFED OXTAIL
QUEUE DE BOEUF FARCIE

Serves 4

2 whole oxtails, chopped into segments
1 tablespoon clarified butter (page 42)
25 g (1 oz) mushrooms, wiped with a
  damp cloth
350 g (12 oz) tomatoes, diced
sea salt
700 ml (1¼ pints) reduced veal stock
  (page 150)
100 g (3½ oz) butter, chilled and
  diced

For the marinade:

250 g (9 oz) red onions, chopped
150 g (5 oz) carrots, chopped
150 g (5 oz) celery, chopped
1 garlic clove
2 cloves
1 bay leaf
2 sprigs of thyme
a few parsley stalks
1 tablespoon black peppercorns
1.5 litres (2½ pints) red wine
3 tablespoons olive oil

For the stuffing:

500 ml (18 fl oz) milk
65 g (2½ oz) butter
sea salt
freshly grated nutmeg
100 g (3½ oz) semolina
2 egg yolks
1 tablespoon freshly grated Parmesan

To serve:

an assortment of vegetables

To make the marinade, mix all the ingredients together in an ovenproof dish large enough to take the oxtail pieces in one layer. Add the meat, pushing it down into the marinade. Leave, covered, for 12 hours.

Remove the oxtail from the marinade and pat dry with kitchen towel. Heat the clarified butter, add the meat and sear on all sides. Strain the marinade, reserving the liquid, then add the vegetables to the oxtail and brown quickly.

Pour in the marinade liquid, add the mushrooms and diced tomatoes, season, then stir in the veal stock. Cook, covered, for about 2 hours in the oven, preheated to 200°C/400°F/gas 6.

Meanwhile make the stuffing: bring the milk to the boil with the butter, a little salt and a generous grating of nutmeg. Sprinkle on the semolina, and stir continuously, and fairly vigorously, until the semolina has absorbed all the liquid. Remove from the heat, then beat in the egg yolks and Parmesan. Transfer to a piping bag with a medium-sized nozzle.

With a slotted spoon, lift the oxtail out of the pan on to a clean work surface and cool slightly. On top of the stove, boil the sauce to reduce to 500 ml (18 fl oz). Carefully remove the centre bones from the pieces of oxtail, retaining their shape as much as possible.

Pipe the semolina stuffing into the bone cavities, and set the meat on an ovenproof plate. Moisten with a little sauce and brown in the oven, preheated to 200°C/400°F/gas 6, for about 10 minutes. Meanwhile, steam the accompanying vegetables.

Strain the reduced sauce through a fine sieve, season, reheat and whisk in the butter a knob at a time, until the sauce is smooth and glossy. Place two stuffed oxtail pieces on each plate, surrounded by a little sauce, and accompanied by the vegetables. Serve any remaining meat separately.

Brown the pieces of meat in the clarified butter, add the marinade vegetables and brown quickly

Pour in the marinade, add the mushrooms, diced tomato and veal stock. Braise for 2 hours . . .

To accompany, try a robust Italian red wine, such as Montepulciano d'Abruzzo or Rosso Cònero

. . . at 200°C/400°F/gas 6. Leave the meat to cool, then take out the bones

Pipe the prepared semolina filling into the bone cavities

CALVES' SWEETBREAD RAVIOLI
RAVIOLI AUX RIS DE VEAU

Serves 4

For the dough:

125 g (4 oz) flour, plus extra for dusting

2 eggs

1 teaspoon oil

1 tablespoon milk

For the filling:

125 g (4 oz) calves' sweetbreads, soaked for at least 4 hours in cold water, blanched for 3 minutes, then membranes removed

sea salt

freshly ground black pepper

For the sauce:

75 g (3 oz) parsley, destalked

300 ml (½ pint) light veal stock (page 150)

2 tablespoons white wine

freshly grated nutmeg

freshly ground black pepper

sea salt

200 ml (7 fl oz) double cream

To garnish:

50 g (2 oz) carrots, peeled, cut into julienne strips and quickly blanched

Sift the flour into a large bowl or on to a clean work surface. Make a well in the middle, break in 1 egg, add the oil and milk then knead thoroughly to form a smooth dough. Pat into a ball and wrap in lightly oiled cling film. Leave to stand for 1 hour.

Chop the sweetbreads fairly finely, season with salt and pepper, then set aside.

Flatten the ball of dough lightly, then pass through the smooth roller of a pasta machine several times to relax it. Or roll out by hand very thinly on a floured work surface. Trim any ragged edges, then cut into strips about 6.5 cm (2½ inches) wide. Lightly beat the other egg, then use to glaze the dough.

Place small heaps of sweetbread, about 2.5 cm (1 inch) apart, on half the strips of dough, covering them with the remaining strips. Press firmly to seal down one long side, then press gently around the filling working towards the open side, pushing all the air out. Now, with a pastry cutter, cut into squares of about 5×5 cm (2×2 inches). Sprinkle with flour, lay on a clean tea towel and cover.

To make the sauce, blanch the parsley in boiling salted water for 1 minute, drain and refresh in iced water. Bring the stock and white wine to the boil, season with nutmeg, pepper and a little salt and reduce by two-thirds. Pour in the cream, add the parsley, thoroughly squeezed of all moisture, and reduce the sauce until thick and creamy. Purée in a food processor or blender, and adjust the seasoning. Return to the pan and keep warm.

Cook the ravioli in boiling salted water for 2–3 minutes until tender – they'll rise to the top. Drain and serve on a pool of the sauce, garnished with strips of carrot.

Lightly brush the strips of dough with beaten egg

Distribute spoonfuls of the filling at regular intervals on half the strips of dough

*To accompany, try a fine northern Italian red wine, such as
Barbaresco or Valtellina Superiore*

Carefully lay another strip of dough on top, and press firmly around the filling to seal the edges

Using a pastry cutter, cut the ravioli into squares of 5×5 cm (2×2 inches). Lightly dust with flour and place on a clean tea towel until required for cooking

CALF'S HEAD WITH TONGUE IN GREEN SAUCE
TÊTE ET LANGUE DE VEAU À LA SAUCE VERTE

Serves 4

½ calf's head, boned and prepared
  (order in advance from the butcher)
1 bay leaf
8 peppercorns
1 small onion
1 clove
a few sprigs of flat parsley
sea salt

For the tongue:

1 small calf's tongue, well rinsed
1 bay leaf
1 small onion
1 clove
5–8 peppercorns
a few sprigs of flat parsley
sea salt

For the sauce:

75 g (3 oz) curly parsley, stalks
  discarded
40 g (1½ oz) flat parsley, stalks
  discarded
125 g (4 oz) pickled gherkins,
  chopped
1 anchovy fillet
1 shallot, finely chopped
8 capers
3 tablespoons red wine vinegar
3 tablespoons olive oil
freshly ground black pepper
sea salt

Bring a large pan with plenty of water to the boil, add the calf's head, and blanch for 3–4 minutes. Cool quickly by plunging in cold water, then chop into small pieces 3–4 cm (1¼–1½ inches) long. Return to the rinsed-out pan, cover with fresh cold water and slowly bring to the boil. Skim off the surface scum, then add the bay leaf, peppercorns, onion studded with the clove, parsley sprigs and a pinch of salt. Simmer gently for about 1½ hours.

Put the tongue into another pan and cover with cold water. Secure the bay leaf to the onion with the clove, add to the pan with the remaining seasoning ingredients and bring to the boil. Skim off the scum, then cook for 40–50 minutes.

Lift the tongue out of the pan, transfer to a large bowl of iced water to cool quickly, then peel off the skin, and trim off any gristly bits. Add a little salt to the cooking liquid, return the tongue to the pan and leave over the gentlest of heats until required for serving.

To make the sauce, purée the parsley in a blender with the pickled gherkins, anchovy fillet, shallot, capers, vinegar and oil. Season with a little pepper, salt if necessary, and divide between four plates.

Drain the pieces of calf's head thoroughly, then the tongue. Slice the tongue thinly and place on top of the sauce with a few pieces of calf's head.

Cover the tongue with cold water, add the seasoning ingredients and bring to the boil

Skim off the scum, then gently simmer for 40–50 minutes

To accompany, try a sturdy Beaujolais cru *wine, such as Moulin-à-Vent or Morgon*

Remove the tongue, put into iced water and peel off the skin

Return the skinned tongue to the simmering broth until just before serving. Drain and cut into slices

POACHED SADDLE OF LAMB
SELLE D'AGNEAU POCHÉE

Serves 4

800 g (1¾ lbs) saddle of lamb, boned out (ask the butcher to chop the bones, and use them for the sauce)

For the stock:

25 g (1 oz) butter
1 celery stalk, washed and chopped
1 small onion, quartered
1 leek, washed and chopped
the lamb bones, chopped, and the trimmings
1 litre (1¾ pints) water
8–10 peppercorns
sea salt

For the vegetables:

75 g (3 oz) red onions
75 g (3 oz) white onions
75 g (3 oz) leeks, washed
100 g (3½ oz) Brussels sprouts, trimmed
75 g (3 oz) savoy cabbage leaves
100 g (3½ oz) butter, softened
sea salt
freshly ground black pepper
1 tablespoon finely snipped chives
1 teaspoon finely chopped basil leaves
1 garlic clove

Carefully trim away all the fat and sinew from the saddle fillets, keeping the trimmings for the stock.

To make the stock, melt the butter, add the vegetables and sweat gently, then add the bones and lamb trimmings and brown lightly. Add the water, peppercorns and a little salt, bring to the boil, then simmer, uncovered, for about 40–45 minutes. Strain the stock through a fine sieve, return to the pan, and reduce by half.

Meanwhile, peel and quarter the red and white onions, then separate into individual layers. Slice the white part of the leek, pull off the Brussels sprout leaves and chop the cabbage leaves into pieces 3×3 cm (1¼×1¼ inches).

Soften the onions and leek in a pan with 1 tablespoon butter, and season with salt. Add the sprout and cabbage leaves, soften briefly and season with pepper. Place the lamb fillets on top of the vegetables and pour over the reduced stock. Bring to the boil, and simmer gently, covered, for about 15 minutes. Then transfer the meat to a warm plate, cover and leave to stand to let the juices rest.

Add the chives and basil to the vegetables, stir in the remaining butter, cook for a minute or two then pierce the garlic clove on a fork and stir through the vegetables several times to impart a light garlic flavour.

Slice the lamb. Spoon a little sauce, and some vegetables, on to four plates, place the lamb on top and add a sprinkling of coarse salt.

Fry the onions and leek in 1 tablespoon hot butter until golden, season with salt

Add the Brussels sprouts and savoy cabbage leaves, lay the meat on top

To accompany, try a fine Médoc Bordeaux from Pauillac,
or a Côte Rôtie

Pour on the reduced lamb stock, cook, covered, for about 15 minutes

Remove the meat. Mix the herbs and butter with the vegetables, pierce the garlic clove with a fork, and stir through the vegetables

GARLIC ROAST LEG OF LAMB

GIGOT D'AGNEAU RÔTI À L'AïL

Serves 6-8

1 leg of lamb, about 1.8 kg (4 lb) in
* weight, skin removed*
1 kg (2 lb) medium-sized potatoes,
* peeled*
6 garlic cloves
coarse sea salt
2 sprigs of thyme
freshly ground black pepper
50 g (2 oz) butter, chilled and diced

Remove the lamb from the refrigerator at least 2 hours before cooking, to bring to room temperature.

Preheat the oven to 220°C/425°F/gas 7. Peel and quarter 4 garlic cloves. Pierce the lamb with the tip of a sharp knife in 16 places and insert a piece of garlic into each incision. Rub the joint all over with a little coarse sea salt.

Place the potatoes around the edges of a large, greased roasting pan with the remaining garlic cloves, unpeeled, and the sprigs of thyme. Season the potatoes with coarse salt and freshly ground pepper, then add the lamb to the tin. Put in the oven and roast for 30-40 minutes per kg (15-20 minutes per pound) for rare meat, 50 minutes per kg (25 minutes per pound) for medium pink lamb, and 1 hour per kg (30 minutes per pound) for well done. At the end of the cooking time, turn off the oven and open the door. Leave the lamb to rest for 15 minutes before carving.

When ready to serve, carve the lamb into slices and arrange on a warmed serving dish surrounded by the potatoes.

Place the roasting tin on the heat, add the diced butter, stir briskly scraping up the sediment in the pan, add a little hot water and stir until smooth. Strain into a hot gravy boat and serve with the lamb.

Pierce the skinned joint with a sharp knife tip, in 16 places, and insert a quarter garlic clove in each incision

Place the lamb in the centre of the potatoes in a large, greased roasting tin – the potatoes having previously been seasoned with sea salt and freshly ground black pepper

To accompany, try a warm, full-bodied bordeaux from Saint-Emilion, or a tasty southern Rhône red, such as Lirac or Gigoudas

When ready to serve, carve the lamb into slices and place on a warmed serving platter

Put the roasting tin on the heat, add the diced butter, stir briskly to scrape up the pan sediments, add a little hot water and stir until smooth

PORK FILLET IN BEER SAUCE
FILET DE PORC SAUCE À LA BIÈRE

Serves 4
450 g (1 lb) pork fillet
sea salt
freshly ground black pepper
1 tablespoon clarified butter (page 42)
1 tablespoon butter
For the sauce:
25 g (1 oz) butter
4 garlic cloves, very lightly crushed
1 tablespoon caraway seeds
100 ml (3½ fl oz) strong brown ale
5 tablespoons brown veal stock (page 150)
sea salt
freshly ground black pepper

Slice the pork evenly into eight pieces, place between two sheets of cling film, flatten lightly with a meat bat and season with a little salt and pepper.

Heat the clarified butter in a frying pan, add the pork and cook for about 3 minutes on each side, until golden brown. Stir in the tablespoon of butter, then remove the meat from the pan and keep warm on a hot plate.

To make the sauce, pour off the pork cooking fat, add a little of the butter to the pan, and gently fry the garlic and caraway seeds. Add the beer, reduce slightly, then add the veal stock and simmer the sauce for 7–8 minutes. Strain through a fine sieve, discarding the garlic and caraway seeds. Return to the pan, beat in the remaining butter, a small knob at a time, and beat well until glossy. Adjust the seasoning.

Place two slices of fillet on each plate, and pour over the beer sauce. White bread dumplings make an excellent accompaniment.

NOTE: Red wine, such as a good *vin de pays,* could be substituted for the ale, and the caraway seeds omitted.

Remove the fried slices of fillet from the pan and pour off the fat

Add a little butter to the sediment in the pan, gently fry the garlic and caraway seeds

*To accompany, try a light Alsace beer, or a fruity young Alsace
white wine such as Pinot Blanc*

Pour on the beer, add the veal stock and
simmer for 7–8 minutes

Strain the sauce into another pan
through a fine sieve, discarding the
garlic and caraway seeds

Pork Goulash
GOULASCH DE PORC

Serves 4
700 g (1 1/2 lbs) shoulder of pork
sea salt
freshly ground black pepper
1 red pepper, halved, all pith and
  seeds removed
5 tablespoons lard
300 g (11 oz) white onions, coarsely
  chopped
3 tablespoons sweet paprika
1 tablespoon tomato purée
500 ml (18 fl oz) brown veal stock
  (page 150)
pinch of ground caraway
700 g (1 1/2 lbs) cooked sauerkraut
150 g (5 oz) crème fraîche, plus extra
  to garnish

Pat the meat dry with kitchen towel, dice coarsely and season with salt and pepper.

Place the halved pepper on a baking sheet, skin side upwards, and roast in the oven at 250°C/500°F/gas 9 for 8–10 minutes. Leave to cool, covered with a damp tea towel, then rub off the skin. Dice the pepper.

Heat the lard in a large pan, add the onions and fry until golden, then season lightly with salt. Add the paprika, half the diced pepper and the tomato purée, and cook until browned, stirring constantly. Add the meat, sear well on all sides, and pour in the stock. Bring to a lively simmer, then stew, very gently, covered, for about 1 hour.

Stir in the caraway and sauerkraut: continue cooking for further 5 minutes, then add the crème fraîche and remaining diced pepper and turn up the heat briefly.

Adjust the seasoning and serve the goulash with an extra dollop of crème fraîche to garnish. Good with boiled potatoes to accompany.

Thoroughly brown the onions, pepper and tomato purée: add the diced meat

Sear the meat all over and pour in the veal stock

To accompany, try a fine dry cider, or an Alsace Gewürztraminer

Stew, covered, for 1 hour. Add the caraway and sauerkraut

Finally stir in the crème fraîche and remaining diced pepper, heat briefly and adjust seasoning

YOUNG PORK LOIN WITH CABBAGE
ÉCHINE DE PORCELET AU CHOU

Serves 4

*1 loin of young pork, about 1 kg (2
  lbs) with rind*
sea salt
freshly ground black pepper
1 small leek
1 large carrot
1 onion
1 tablespoon lard
1 small cabbage
8 tablespoons white wine
*200 ml (7 fl oz) brown veal stock
  (page 150)*

For the basil paste:

*100 g (3½ oz) unsmoked ham,
  minced*
25 g (1 oz) basil leaves
1 garlic clove
*5–6 sprigs of chervil leaves, chopped
  and stalks discarded*
½ teaspoon dried thyme
sea salt

Score the rind of the loin with a knife, trim the skin and fat off the tips of the bones, and season the meat. Wash the leek, carrot and onion, dice coarsely and fry gently in a roasting pan in hot lard.

Set the loin in the roasting pan, skin side down, fry briefly and turn. Then roast for 30–40 minutes in the oven heated to 220°C/425°F/gas 7. Meanwhile, pound all ingredients for the basil paste in a mortar and pestle, or blend in a food processor, to a creamy paste.

Discard the outer, and any damaged, leaves from the cabbage, then chop into small pieces, about 3×3 cm (1¼×1¼ inches), and blanch in boiling salted water for 7–8 minutes. Drain thoroughly, then return to the pan and mix in the basil paste. Season with pepper and keep warm.

Moisten the roast with the white wine, then transfer the meat from the pan to a warm dish and leave to stand. Add the stock to the roasting pan, reduce slightly, and pour the sauce through a sieve. Season with salt and pepper.

To serve, slice the roast into individual chops, place two on a bed of cabbage on each plate and pour over a little sauce.

Lightly fry the pieces of leek, carrot and onion in hot lard

Set the loin in the roasting pan, skin side down, fry lightly and turn over

*To accompany, try a characterful red or white Côtes du Rhône
Villages, or a red wine from Anjou*

Roast at 220°C/425°F/gas 7 for 30 to 40
minutes, then moisten with white wine

Remove the loin from the roasting
pan, leave to stand for 5–10 minutes to
let the juices rest. Cut into individual
chops before serving

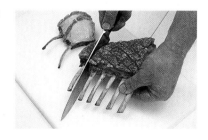

Glazed Gammon
JAMBON FUMÉ GLACÉ

Serves 4–6

*1.2 kg (2 ¾ lbs) gammon leg joint
  with rind, lightly smoked and cured
2 tablespoons runny honey
about 40 cloves
1 tablespoon icing sugar*

For the sauce:

*200 ml (7 fl oz) Madeira
1 small shallot, finely chopped
3 tablespoons white wine
3 tablespoons red wine
400 ml (14 fl oz) brown veal stock
  (page 150)
50 g (2 oz) butter, chilled and diced
sea salt
freshly ground black pepper*

For the corn cakes:

*75 g (3 oz) butter
250 g (9 oz) fresh corn kernels (6–8
  corn cobs)
2 tablespoons flour
200 ml (7 fl oz) double cream
2 eggs
sea salt
freshly ground nutmeg*

Put the gammon joint in a large pan, pour on cold water to cover, and bring to the boil. Lower the heat and simmer for about 1–1½ hours.

Remove the joint from the pan (keep the stock for soup), drain, and cut away the rind. Score the fat in a diamond pattern and coat the surface with honey. Insert a clove in the centre of each diamond and set the joint on a baking sheet. Heat the oven to 200°C/400°F/gas 6, and bake the gammon for about 30 minutes, dredging with icing sugar halfway through cooking time. The honey and icing sugar give the ham a beautiful shiny glaze and a sweet succulent flavour. Check after 20 minutes that it is not browning too quickly, covering with aluminium foil if necessary.

To make the sauce, put the Madeira and shallot into a pan, bring to the boil, add the white and red wines and reduce by half. Pour in the stock, and again reduce by half. Set aside.

To make the corn cakes, melt half the butter, add the corn kernels and fry gently until softened. Purée half the mixture in a food processor. Mix together the flour and double cream, stir in the eggs, the corn purée and the whole kernels. Season with salt and nutmeg, then form into small, flat rounds.

Melt the remaining butter, and fry the corn cakes in batches. Transfer on to kitchen towel to drain off excess fat, and keep warm.

Reheat the sauce, then beat in the butter, a knob at a time, to thicken. Adjust the seasoning. Before serving, remove the cloves from the ham, slice the meat and serve with the corn cakes and sauce.

Carefully cut away the rind from the boiled, drained ham

Score the fat diagonally to give a diamond pattern, coat with honey

To accompany, try a light Médoc Bordeaux from Margaux or
Saint-Julien

Insert a clove in the centre of each diamond, place the joint on a baking sheet

Bake for about 30 minutes at 200°C/400°F/gas 6. Halfway through baking, take the joint out of the oven and dredge with icing sugar

STUFFED PIG'S TROTTER
PIEDS DE PORC FARCIS

Serves 4

1 stuffed pig's trotter, Zampone,
available from Italian delicatessen
(often sold in vacuum sealed bags: if
not, wrap in several thicknesses of
foil and seal tightly)
4–5 tablespoons olive oil
chopped parsley

For the beans:

450 g (1 lb) white haricot beans,
soaked overnight in cold water
75 g (3 oz) diced carrot, celery, leek
1 small shallot, finely chopped
3 tablespoons red wine vinegar
sea salt
freshly ground black pepper
few sprigs of flat parsley, chopped
6 tablespoons olive oil

Drain the beans, rinse in cold running water then cook in lightly salted boiling water for about 1 hour, until tender, adding the diced vegetables about 10 minutes before the end of the cooking time. Drain, and turn into a dish.

Mix the chopped shallot with the vinegar, salt, pepper, parsley and olive oil. Pour over the beans and leave to marinate for 2–3 hours.

Put the wrapped and well sealed pig's trotter into a pan of boiling water, and simmer for about 20 minutes. Remove and cool slightly then cut open the wrapping. Pour the cooking juices in the bag on to the beans and stir. Unwrap the pig's trotter and slice thinly.

Divide the beans between four plates, top with a couple of slices of pig's trotter and sprinkle with the olive oil and the chopped parsley.

Put the pig's trotter in its vacuum sealed bag (otherwise wrapped in foil and tightly sealed) into boiling water and simmer for about 20 minutes

Mix the cooked beans with the marinade and leave to stand for 2–3 hours

*To accompany, try a rustic wine from South-West France
such as Cahors or Madiran*

Unwrap the cooled pig's trotter; pour
the juices on to the beans

Cut the pig's trotter into slices

POULTRY AND GAME

TODAY WE TEND TO THINK OF POULTRY, particularly the chicken, as everyday food, and game as a luxury. Yet for centuries the reverse was rather truer. Game, since very early days, had provided the poor man with much – if not all – of his fresh meat, albeit often illegitimately (though the nobleman was just as likely to be poaching a disliked neighbour's venison as the peasant his master's rabbits). Hares, which are nowadays highly regarded, were the common man's hunting, rarely appearing on the banquet table and certainly never as the honoured dishes that rabbit and coney (a rabbit under one year) provided.

It may seem odd to us that the rabbit should be so desired, until one remembers that the creature had disappeared from many parts of Britain and Europe along with the Roman conquerors on their return home. Well aware of the breeding problems, they had confined them so efficiently in their *leporaria* (hare gardens), that rabbits had largely ceased to exist in the wild. In Elizabethan times, the lord of the manor still had his rabbit warrens, thus ownership of the rabbits, although the animal was increasingly establishing itself in the wild. The native hare, on the other hand, had the freedom of the land – and the peasant the freedom to hunt him.

Certain feathered game was even more desirable (and even less accessible). Pheasant and partridge were both kept in enclosures attached to the manor houses, to be hunted with goshawks, the gentleman's hunting bird. There was little chance for the poacher to enjoy them until the eighteenth century, with the establishment of game woods on the large estates. Then at least it was a possible prey, although a dangerous pursuit: the penalties if caught were still brutally harsh.

Most of primitive man's feathered game was, in fact, provided by the duck and the goose. By Caesar's time, they had become domesticated (the goose to such an extent that in certain areas it was taboo as a food, regarded more as a village mascot). Despite domestication, it still fell into the category of game, though by medieval times it was firmly established as a table creature. In Britain those who could afford it, enjoyed a green goose (one fed on the stubble of the fields after harvesting – thus plump but lean) at the festival of Michaelmas on 29 September. It was traditional, too, to present one's landlord with a goose, along with the payment of the quarterly or annual rent due on that day.

On the Continent, the goose provided the festive dish for Martinmas (11 November), in remembrance of St Martin. Legend recalls that his reluctance to be elected Bishop of Tours drove him to hide in a goose shed, only to be betrayed by the cackling. Whereupon he promptly despatched them to the cooking pot. Geese, indeed, make excellent watchmen, and these large birds are still used as such in some of the more rural areas.

The less fortunate had to wait until Christmas for the goose to appear on their tables (often stuffed with a rabbit to make it stretch further). By the early eighteenth century, the goose had become common Christmas fare.

Turkeys, too, were a familiar sight by then, but they were a more recent farmyard fowl. A native originally of Mexico and Central America, the Spanish Conquistadores had introduced them to Europe around 1523. The first written reference to them in England appears in 1541, when Henry VIII's zealous Archbishop Cranmer declared them one of the 'greater fowls'. This was not in praise of the turkey, but a move to stamp out the gluttonous habits of certain highly placed clerics. Forthwith only one 'great' fowl was permitted per dish. By 1555, they were being widely sold in London, and came within the price regulations on poultry: 6 shillings for a turkey-cock, 2 shillings and 8 pence for the chicks. Archbishop Cranmer would undoubtedly not have approved the famous eighteenth century York Christmas Pie. A turkey, stuffed with a goose, stuffed with a fowl (a hen), then a partridge, and a pigeon (all boned), was placed in a pie crust of 'good standing', then packed on either side with chopped hare meat, 'woodcocks, moor game, and what sort of wildfowl you can get'. Seasoning and four pounds of butter were added to the pie which was then covered with a lid ('which must be a very thick one') before baking. Ancestor to today's Christmas hampers, they were 'often sent to London in a box as presents'.

If turkey was luxurious, so too was chicken, so much so in medieval France, in fact, that St Louis had his own henhouses, covered by royal decree, and the Church ruled the bird 'too good' for a fast day meat.

Henri IV of Navarre (1553–1610) gained popularity by virtuously declaiming that every Frenchman should have 'a chicken in his pot' of a Sunday, a promise he sadly failed to deliver. Chickens held on to their honourable status as a banqueting dish until the turn of the last century. Since then its standing has unhappily declined. Yet today, with the demand for leaner, healthier meats, it is the ideal bird. All too often, however, it is simply a tasteless, frozen product off some battery line. 'It is important for chickens to be free range. The ideal weight for slaughtering is somewhere between 1.6-2kg (3½-4½lbs). There are hundreds of different ways to prepare them, but as so often, the simplest way is the best. Spit-roasted above a wood fire, served with young green peas – the wonderful spring meal.'

Bocuse himself uses the beautiful golden-fleshed, blue-legged chickens from Bresse. The maize they feed upon give them that intense colour – and flavour. Bocuse adds drama in the serving with embers from the fire, above which they have been cooked, glowing on the plate around them.

CHICKEN IN RED WINE
POULET AU VIN ROUGE

Serves 4

1 oven-ready chicken, about 1.5 kg
(3 lbs 5 oz)

For the marinade:

1 onion, peeled

1 celery stalk, washed

1 leek, washed

1 carrot, washed

1 bay leaf

2–3 cloves

sprig of thyme

8 white peppercorns

sprig of parsley

400 ml (14 fl oz) red Burgundy

For the sauce:

salt and pepper

5 tablespoons vegetable oil

700 ml (1 1/4 pints) brown chicken
stock (page 149)

1 small garlic clove, chopped

3 small tomatoes, skinned and diced

50 g (2 oz) butter, chilled and diced

To garnish:

10 g (scant 1/2 oz) dried boletus,
soaked in warm water

1 tablespoon butter

50 g (2 oz) green bacon in one piece,
derinded and diced

12 pearl onions, peeled

sea salt

4 slices of white bread

65 g (2 1/2 oz) clarified butter (page
42)

finely chopped parsley

Rinse the chicken well, then dry with kitchen towel. Using a cleaver or sharp, heavy knife, cut off the thighs, then cut down the breast close to the bone and detach first one, then the other breast from the carcass. Cut off the wings, then chop off the small, meaty end wing joints – put those with the breasts and legs, add the tips to the carcass to make the stock.

For the marinade, dice the vegetables finely, mix in a bowl with the chicken pieces, herbs and Burgundy and leave, covered, for 24 hours to marinate.

Remove the chicken from the marinade, dry well and season with salt and pepper. Heat the oil in a large pan, add the chicken pieces and sear quickly. Strain the marinade, keeping the liquid, and adding the vegetables to the meat. Cook for a minute or so over a high heat, then pour off the oil. Add the marinade to the pan, let bubble for a minute, then add the chicken stock, garlic and tomatoes, bring to the boil, then lower the heat and gently simmer for 20–30 minutes. Remove the meat from the pan and keep warm on a plate over a pan of simmering water.

Raise the heat and reduce the sauce to about half, then purée in a blender or push through a sieve, mashing as much of the vegetable pulp as possible. Return to the pan and reheat without boiling while adding the butter, whisking well between each addition. Correct the seasoning if necessary, then keep warm.

For the garnish, drain the boletus, squeezing to remove excess moisture, then chop. Melt the butter and sweat the mushrooms, bacon and pearl onions for a few minutes, salting lightly. Cut out eight heart shapes from the bread, melt the clarified butter and quickly fry the croûtons until golden on both sides. Drain and sprinkle with parsley.

Serve the chicken, with some sauce poured over and garnished with a few vegetables and two heart croûtons.

Mix the chicken pieces, vegetables and red wine and marinate, covered, for 24 hours

Sear the drained and seasoned chicken pieces in hot oil

To accompany, try a robust red Burgundy from the Côte Chalonnaise, such as Mercurey or Givry

Moisten with the marinade

Add the chicken stock, garlic and tomatoes, then simmer gently for about 20–30 minutes

Stuffed Spring Chicken
POUSSIN FARCI

Serves 4
1 oven-ready spring chicken, about
1.3 kg (2 lbs 14 oz) drawn weight,
plus the giblets
sea salt
freshly ground black pepper
For the stuffing:
250 g (9 oz) butter
1 shallot, finely chopped
liver and heart of the chicken, minced
(if you were given the neck in the
giblets, keep that for stock)
3–4 morels, chopped and washed (see
Note)
1 tablespoon finely chopped chervil
1 tablespoon finely chopped parsley
2 small sprigs of rosemary
sea salt
freshly ground black pepper
175 g (6 oz) white bread, crusts
removed, then diced
1 egg
freshly grated nutmeg
1 tablespoon finely chopped marjoram

First make the stuffing: melt 25 g (1 oz) butter, add the shallot and sweat for a few minutes. Add the minced chicken liver and heart, the morels, chervil, parsley and rosemary and cook for a further 5–6 minutes. Season lightly with salt and pepper, cover and keep aside.

Melt about 150 g (5 oz) butter in a frying pan, add 100 g (3½ oz) of the diced bread and fry until crisp and golden. Place on kitchen towel to drain.

Mash the rest of the butter to lightly soften, gradually whisk in the egg, beating until well blended, then stir in the unfried bread. Add the chicken liver/mushroom mixture, having first removed the rosemary sprig – reserve the rosemary. Season with salt, pepper and freshly grated nutmeg, then add the marjoram and fried bread cubes.

Gently loosen the chicken skin over the breastbone, being careful not to tear it. Insert a layer of stuffing under the skin, allowing room for expansion – too much may cause the skin to split in the cooking. Season the inside of the bird with salt and pepper, then fill with any remaining stuffing plus the rosemary sprig. Cover the neck end opening with the skin and sew with kitchen cotton or string to seal, then truss the bird to keep it in shape during cooking. Place in a roasting tin, add a cupful of water and roast in the oven, preheated to 180°C/350°F/gas 4, for 1–1½ hours. Baste it from time to time with the pan juices, and cover with foil after about 50 minutes if necessary to avoid over-browning.

Transfer the bird to a warmed platter and pour the juices into a tall jug. Carve down the breast so that each slice is topped with some stuffing. Skim the gravy of any fat, then serve the breast meat on warm plates with a little gravy poured over, and the thighs handed round separately. Gratin potatoes make a good accompaniment.

NOTE: If you have fresh morels (March-May is their season) chop *before* washing in salted water to remove insects as well as earth from the honeycomb-like surface. If the fresh fungus is unavailable use canned or dried.

Insert your thumbs between the breast flesh and skin to loosen the skin

Push your hand in gently, being careful not to tear the skin

*To accompany, try a full-bodied white Graves, or an aged
Australian Sémillon*

Using a tablespoon, insert stuffing
between the skin and flesh

Pull the skin at the neck end over the
stuffing, and sew with kitchen cotton to
seal. Truss the bird to keep in shape
during cooking

Turkey Breast Fillets in Vegetable Jackets
FILETS DE BLANC DE DINDE ENVELOPPÉS DE LÉGUMES

Serves 4

400 g (14 oz) turkey breast fillets
sea salt
freshly ground black pepper
1 tablespoon clarified butter (page 42)
125 g (4 oz) turkey giblets, washed, all yellow pieces cut out of the liver, then giblets finely chopped
100 g (3½ oz) mushrooms, wiped clean with a damp cloth
100 g (3½ oz) spinach leaves, washed
25 g (1 oz) parsley, stalks removed
100 ml (3½ fl oz) double cream
1 egg
large piece caul fat, soaked (see Note)

Divide the turkey breast into four equal pieces and season lightly with salt and pepper. Melt the butter, add the meat and brown on both sides quickly. Remove from the pan and leave to cool.

Add the chopped giblets to the pan, slice the mushrooms finely, then add together with the spinach, parsley and a light sprinkling of salt and pepper. Cover and simmer for 5–6 minutes. Transfer to a blender, add 1 tablespoon double cream and purée coarsely. Pour into a bowl, set over another bowl of iced water, and stir until cool. Then stir in the egg and the remaining double cream, little by little, until you have a thick and smooth mixture. Check the seasoning and adjust if necessary.

Spread out the caul fat and cut into four even-sized pieces. Make a layer of the purée the same shape and size as the turkey pieces on each piece of fat, lay a turkey fillet on top and cover with more purée. Wrap around the caul, bringing over the long edges first, then tucking the short sides underneath. Place the parcels in a roasting pan and cook in the oven, preheated to 190°C/375°F/gas 5 for 20 minutes – the fat should have formed a deep golden-brown webbing.

To serve, cut each fillet into slices, arrange on warmed plates and, if wished, pour over a little of the pan juices.

NOTE: Caul fat is the lace-like membrane that lines part of the abdominal cavity in certain animals – pig's caul is commonly used in cooking to cover faggots, and *crepinettes* and *gayettes* in France. Before using, soak in warm water with a pinch of salt or vinegar, to soften. It can then be stretched easily without tearing.

Spread out the softened caul fat and make a layer of purée on it

Place the cooled turkey breast on top and cover with more purée

*To accompany, try a light red Burgundy from the Hautes Côtes de
Beaune, or an Alsace Pinot Noir*

Trim the caul so that it will wrap neatly
round the fillet

Wrap the parcels, folding over the long
edges first, then tucking the short sides
underneath. Arrange in a roasting tin

75

DUCK À L'ORANGE
CANARD À L'ORANGE

Serves 4

*1 oven-ready duckling, about 3 kg
  (6 lbs 10 oz), with its giblets*
sea salt
freshly ground black pepper
3 tablespoons vegetable oil
1 small onion, finely diced
1 carrot, washed and diced
1 celery stalk, washed and diced
100 ml (3½ fl oz) red wine
*125 ml (4 fl oz) chicken stock (page
  149)*

For the sauce:

1 tablespoon butter
2 tablespoons sugar
*about 125 ml (4 fl oz) red wine
  vinegar*
*100 ml (3½ fl oz) veal stock (page
  150)*
juice of 3 oranges
juice of 3 lemons
*zest of 1 orange, cut into julienne
  strips*
*zest of 1 lemon, cut into julienne
  strips (both fruits washed well first)*
*50–65 g (2–2½ oz) butter, chilled
  and flaked*

To garnish:

segments of 4 oranges, skinned

Rinse the duck in cold water, dry well and season the inside with salt and pepper. Truss if wished, then place in a roasting pan, together with the giblets and about a cupful of water. Brush the skin with oil then roast in the oven, preheated to 200°C/400°F/gas 6 for about 30 minutes, basting occasionally with the pan juices.

Remove the duck from the roasting tin (draining off any juices inside the duck back into the pan) and keep warm. Skim the fat off the pan juices, then add the diced vegetables and roast for 5–6 minutes. Transfer the pan to the top of the stove, add the red wine and bubble for a minute, then pour in the stock and bubble hard to reduce by half.

Meanwhile, in a separate pan, melt the butter, add the sugar and stir until caramelized to a golden brown. Add the vinegar, veal stock, orange and lemon juices and boil to reduce by half. Strain the gravy in the roasting pan (discard the vegetables), skim off any fat, then add to the orange sauce. Stir in the julienne of orange and lemon zests, and simmer fairly vigorously to further reduce the sauce until thick and syrupy. Whisk the butter into the sauce to make it beautifully glossy, then add the orange segments and heat through quickly.

Carve the duck breast thinly (cook the legs a little more and keep for another recipe), arrange on warmed plates with a little sauce, and a few orange segments to the side.

Melt the butter, add the sugar and stir until caramelized

Stir continuously to prevent the sugar crystallizing and over-browning

To accompany, try an assertive red wine, such as an Italian Barbera
or a Californian Zinfandel

Add the vinegar, stock, orange and
lemon juices and reduce by half

Add the julienned zests, reduce further,
then stir in flakes of cold butter. Briefly
warm the orange segments in the sauce

77

ROAST GOOSE WITH SEMOLINA DUMPLINGS
OIE RÔTIE AUX BOULETTES À LA SEMOULE

Serves 4

1 young oven-ready goose, about 2.5 kg (5½ lbs)
sea salt
1 medium-sized dessert apple
1 onion
1 sprig of tarragon
250 ml (9 fl oz) water
400 ml (14 fl oz) brown chicken stock (page 149)

For the dumplings:

150 g (5 oz) butter
4 eggs
250 g (9 oz) semolina
5 bread rolls, about 200 g (7 oz) total weight, crusts removed, then finely diced
125 ml (4 fl oz) soured cream
450 g (1 lb) potatoes, preferably King Edward, or another floury variety, scrubbed
sea salt
freshly grated nutmeg

For the baked apples:

4 dessert apples, preferably russets or Cox's, washed
40 g (1½ oz) butter
2 tablespoons cranberries, defrosted if frozen
3 tablespoons sugar
juice of half a lemon
2 tablespoons white wine

Rinse the goose, pat dry, cut off excess fatty bits by the vent, then season inside with salt. Peel, halve and core the apple, stuff into the goose together with the onion and tarragon. Pour the water into a large roasting pan, bring to the boil on top of the stove, then lower in the goose.

Cook for approximately 1½–2 hours in the oven, preheated to 220°C/425°F/gas 7. Baste frequently with the cooking juices. After an hour, remove the stuffing from the goose, and place in the roasting pan. Return to the oven.

To make the semolina dumplings, beat the butter until very creamy, then add the eggs one by one, beating well between each addition, then add the semolina. Leave the egg and semolina mixture to stand for about 1 hour.

Steep the diced bread in the soured cream to soften. Boil the potatoes until quite soft, peel, chop coarsely and lay out on a baking sheet. Put into the oven, lower the heat to 200°C/400°F/gas 6, and dry out for 5–7 minutes. Push through a coarse sieve so they are totally lump-free, then season with salt and nutmeg, and mix very thoroughly. Work into the semolina dough.

Remove the goose from the roasting pan and keep warm on a plate over a large pan of simmering water. Add the stock to the pan, boil vigorously and pour through a fine sieve. If necessary, skim off the fat, and adjust seasoning to taste.

Form the dough into small dumplings and drop gently into boiling salted water; cook for about 15 minutes.

Meanwhile, core the apples, place in a lightly buttered, ovenproof dish, fill the cavities with cranberries and sprinkle with sugar, dotting the remaining butter on top. Bake in the oven at the highest heat for 20 minutes. Add the lemon juice and wine and cook for a further few minutes until the juice has reduced to a thick sauce.

To serve, carve the goose and serve with the semolina dumplings and baked apples, pouring a little gravy over the meat, the apple sauce over the apples.

Stuff the goose with the apple halves, onion and tarragon

Bring the water to the boil in a roasting pan, place the goose in the pan and cook for 1½ to . . .

*To accompany, try a fine red Loire Bourgueil or Chinon, or an
Oregon Pinot Noir*

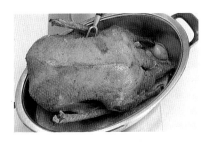

. . . 2 hours at 220°C/425°F/gas 7. Lift
the cooked goose out of the roasting
pan and drain off the fat.

Before serving, carve the goose. Remove
the breast meat in one piece, then carve,
at a slight angle, into slices. Cut off
the legs

STUFFED QUAIL WITH KALE

QUAILLES FARCIES AU CHOU

Serves 4

4 oven-ready quail, boned (ask the
   butcher to bone them from the back
   – although one can do it at home,
   it's a fiddly job unless you're very
   experienced)
freshly ground black pepper
sea salt
1 piece of caul fat, soaked in tepid
   water, then cut into 4

For the kale:

1 kg (2 lbs) kale
40 g (1½ oz) smoked bacon, diced
1 small onion, finely chopped
1 garlic clove, finely chopped
a few marjoram leaves
a few sprigs of parsley, chopped
freshly grated nutmeg
sea salt
freshly ground black pepper

For the stuffing:

25 g (1 oz) butter
75 g (3 oz) chicken livers, trimmed of
   any yellowish pieces, then diced
1 small apple, peeled, cored and diced
50 g (2 oz) good white bread, crust
   removed and diced
5 tablespoons double cream
1 teaspoon finely chopped parsley
a few thyme leaves
freshly grated nutmeg
freshly ground black pepper
sea salt

Strip the kale leaves off the stalks, wash thoroughly and chop coarsely. Blanch for 2 minutes in boiling salted water, refresh in cold water, drain thoroughly, then squeeze to rid of excess moisture.

Briefly fry the bacon in a large pan, add the onion and garlic, cook for a minute, then add the kale, marjoram and parsley.

Season with nutmeg, salt and pepper and cook, covered, for about 20 minutes.

To make the stuffing, melt the butter, add the chicken livers and diced apple, and fry for 2–3 minutes. Add the remaining stuffing ingredients together with 2–3 tablespoons of the kale. Stir well to mix, adjust the seasoning and leave to cool.

Carefully rinse the quail in cold water, pat dry with kitchen towel, then lightly season the insides with salt and pepper. Fill with the prepared stuffing, press the quails into shape, and wrap each in a piece of caul fat. Place in a roasting pan and roast in the oven, preheated to 190°C/375°F/gas 5, for about 20 minutes, until beautifully golden.

Drain off the quail cooking juices, stir them into the kale, then serve each quail on a bed of kale.

Lay the boned quail on a work surface, back side up, and fill with the stuffing

Draw up the skin to cover the stuffing, hold the skin tightly closed (or secure with a cocktail stick if wished), then turn the bird over

To accompany, try a tasty southern French red wine, such as a good
Minervois or Corbières

Carefully press the stuffed quails back
into their original shape

Then wrap each quail in a piece of caul
fat and set in a roasting pan

PARTRIDGE BREASTS WITH MUSHROOMS
BLANCS DE PERDRIX AUX CHAMPIGNONS

Serves 4

*4 young oven-ready partridges (ask
the butcher to cut off the breasts,
and use the carcasses and legs for the
stock)*

sea salt

freshly ground black pepper

2 tablespoons butter

*4 tablespoons very reduced, brown
chicken stock (page 149, but using
the partridge carcasses)*

½ teaspoon sweet paprika

200 ml (7 fl oz) double cream

For the mushrooms:

*250 g (9 oz) mushrooms, wiped clean
with a damp cloth*

50 g (2 oz) butter

sea salt

freshly ground black pepper

To garnish:

chervil leaves

Lightly season the partridge breasts on both sides with salt and pepper then fry, skin side first, in hot butter; turn and finish frying on the other side. The breasts should still be pink inside. Remove the meat from the pan and keep warm.

Add the reduced stock and the paprika to the pan, then stir in the double cream and reduce until thick and smooth. Meanwhile, slice the mushrooms, melt the butter and add the mushrooms, cooking briefly to soften. Season with salt and pepper. Drain, and add to the sauce just to heat through.

Cut the breasts at a slight angle into 1 cm (½ inch) thick slices, and serve with the mushroom sauce, garnished with chervil leaves.

Season the partridge breasts on both
sides with salt and pepper

Fry in hot butter, skin side first, then
turn and fry the other side until done

*To accompany, try a red Burgundy from the Côtes de Beaune, or a
red Rioja Reserva*

To serve, cut the breasts into slices,
about 1 cm (½ inch) thick

Heat the drained mushrooms in the
sauce

HARE ROYALE
LIÈVRE À LA ROYALE

Serves 4

2 fresh hares, about 1.5 kg (3 lbs)
   each in weight, skinned and
   paunched by the butcher, blood and
   liver reserved, the blood mixed with
   1 teaspoon vinegar to prevent
   coagulation
2 tablespoons cognac
20 thin slices pork back fat, 10×25
   cm (4×10 inches) each
1 large carrot, washed
1 bay leaf
3 cloves
3 onions, peeled but left whole
15 shallots, peeled but left whole
10 garlic cloves, unpeeled
1 sprig of thyme
1 sprig of parsley
sea salt
freshly ground black pepper
250 ml (9 fl oz) red wine vinegar
2 bottles red Burgundy

Remove the bluish, thin membrane which holds the joints of the hare together, carefully slitting at one point with a thin, sharp knife and then sliding the knife underneath so that you can pull the membranes off easily. Blot the hare dry with kitchen towel, then fold the forelegs against the chest, the backlegs against the stomach and truss to keep in shape during cooking.

Chop the liver finely, cutting out any yellowish bits as they will taste bitter, then mix with the blood and cognac and keep aside.

Line a flameproof casserole dish with the pork fat, using a couple of slices to cover the base, then overlapping the rest around the sides, with a slight overlap at the top of the dish. Place the hare in the dish.

Dice the carrot and strew over the hare; secure the bay leaf with the cloves on to one of the onions, then tuck the onions, shallots and garlic around the hare. Add the herbs, a light sprinkling of salt, more of pepper, then fold the fat over the hare to completely encase. Pour in the vinegar and 1½ bottles Burgundy. Cover, bring to the boil, then reduce the heat as low as possible and stew, very gently, for 3 hours.

Remove the hare from the dish carefully and put on a hot plate, keep warm. Sieve the pan juices, remove the bay leaf and cloves from the onion, squeeze the garlic out of its skins, purée the vegetables in a blender with a little gravy, stir in the rest of the gravy, then return to the heat. Add the remaining wine, stir well and boil to reduce and thicken. Add the liver, blood and cognac, mashing the gravy until very smooth, but without letting it boil or it will curdle. Adjust the seasoning if necessary and keep hot in a bain-marie.

Remove the string from the hare, and lift the meat off the bones. Arrange on a warmed serving platter, pour over the gravy and serve at once. Noodles and Brussels sprouts are good accompaniments.

Line a large, flameproof casserole with the pork back fat

Put in the trussed hare, strewing the vegetables, herbs and seasoning around the meat

To accompany, try a fine red Burgundy from the Côte de Nuits, such
as a Morey-Saint-Denis or Nuits-Saint-Georges Premier Cru

Fold over the pork fat to encase the
hare, then cover with 2–3 more slices
of fat

Add the vinegar, 1½ bottles of
Burgundy, then cover, bring to the boil
and stew gently for 3 hours

VEGETABLES

SOME THIRTY YEARS AGO, ON THE regular New Year card Bocuse sends to his friends, was included a recipe for the pumpkin. With the top sliced off, the seeds scooped out, it is then three-quarters filled with layers of croûtons and grated Gruyère, seasoned, and topped up with cream. After two hours in a hot oven, the giant soup bowl is brought bubbling and golden to the table. Magical treatment for the magical vegetable; a vegetable whose precise origin is in some dispute among botanists, though most assert it to be American.

Indisputedly from America (South America however, not Virginia as claimed by John Gerard) comes another vegetable much loved by Bocuse. 'For me the queen of winter vegetables is the potato. This tuber is unjustly regarded as inferior by many people. In our restaurant we deliberately serve many potato dishes. A plain baked potato with salmon, a good purée, various gratins. One of our most popular dishes is red mullet with the scales replaced by a layer of thinly sliced potato in which it is fried. A refined dish, although basically there is nothing more on the plate than fish and fried potatoes.'

Such refinement did not come to the potato, however, for nearly two hundred years after its introduction to Europe. (Sweet potatoes were another matter. Much lauded and written about, enjoyed by Henry VIII, they had been a culinary success since their appearance on Columbus' return to Spain after his voyage of discovery.) Who first brought the true potato to Europe is not definite, but certainly Sir Francis Drake was among the earliest importers. He took some abroad at Columbia, stopped at Virginia on his way home to England (hence Gerard's confusion) and praised them lavishly. Still they were slow to find favour. Walter Raleigh apparently grew them on his Irish estate, and presented some to the English queen, Elizabeth 1. The story goes that the royal chef cooked the leaves, consigning the tubers to the bin. The Queen was not impressed. And neither, until the late eighteenth century, were many others. Food for cattle they definately were, and occasionally for the poor (though even in 1750, Frederick William I of Prussia had to send troops to guard the potato fields, so bent on their destruction were the peasants he was trying to feed), but certainly not for the rich.

Only, curiously, in Switzerland was the potato appreciated. Two brothers, Jean and Gaspard Bauhin were fascinated by the plants sent to them from Peru in 1590: they grew them, studied them, wrote about them, and named them – *solanum tuberosum esculentum*. Minus the last word, that is still their botanical name today. It is not surprising then that also from Switzerland, in 1598, came a cookery book (believed to be the first by a woman) with one of the earliest recipes we have for potatoes – *kartoffelrösti*. A dish, of course, still popular today, and Bocuse makes his *rösti* even more sumptious with a puff pastry crust.

He also marries the humble tuber to exotica; potato fritters with snails, baked potatoes extravagantly stuffed, a potato soup flavoured with cèpes. The essence of these dishes is an unusual combination and, perhaps more importantly, a lavish hand with rich seasonings – for this 'winter vegetable ... you shouldn't stint on the butter and cream'.

The delicacies of spring, on the contrary, 'such as the first small peas, are best prepared completely pure'. Unlike the potato, the pea had long been known and appreciated. 'I have fresh peas in the pod' was a familiar thirteenth century Paris street cry and, in the seventeenth century, 'Greens peas for Lent, as sweet as cream'. At Court, they were all the rage: 'The subject of peas is being treated at length: impatience to eat them, the pleasure of having eaten them, and the longing to eat them again are the three points about which our princes have been talking for four days', wrote Madame de Maintenoy on 10 May 1695. Even the Sun King suffered the indignity of appalling indigestion one night after gross over-indulgence.

Perhaps Madame de Pompadour, mistress to his successor, recalled the occasion for she indulged not in dishes of petit pois, but asparagus – dipped into soft-boiled egg yolks, an aid apparently, to her boudoir prowess. Bocuse combines it, less romantically but most deliciously, with tender calves' brains as an early summer salad.

As summer progresses, the market stalls are piled high with fresh produce: the new shoots of spinach, herbs in abundance, pencil slim leeks, radishes, gleaming aubergines, crisp French beans, broad beans so young and tender they can be eaten raw, tiny courgettes with their flowers – golden trumpets ideal for stuffing. Young and unblemished, and very fresh and smelling of the sun, treated simply in the manner of Bocuse, these fruits of the garden and field are worthy of being presented as a course on their own.

Asparagus and Calves' Brain Salad
SALADE D'ASPERGES ET DE CERVELLE DE VEAU

Serves 4
700 g (1½ lbs) white asparagus
sea salt
pinch of sugar
1 slice white bread

For the salad dressing:
¼–½ teaspoon Dijon mustard
1 egg yolk
sea salt
1 small shallot, finely chopped
2 tablespoons red wine vinegar
2 tablespoons raspberry vinegar
2 tablespoons balsam vinegar
2 tablespoons reduced veal stock (page 150)
200 ml (7 fl oz) grapeseed oil
2–3 tablespoons double cream

For the brains:
400 g (14 oz) calves' brains
sea salt
freshly ground black pepper
flour for dusting
40 g (1½ oz) butter

To garnish:
a few small leaves of lamb's lettuce, washed
40 g (1½ oz) pearl barley, fried in a little oil until soft
chopped parsley or chervil

First, place the brains in plenty of cold water and leave to soak for several hours.

Peel the asparagus, starting about 2 cm (¾ inch) below the tip. Cut off the woody ends. Plunge the asparagus into lightly salted boiling water, to which you have added a pinch of sugar and the slice of bread (the bread absorbs the cooking smells). Cook for about 15 minutes – but take care not to overdo. Cool the asparagus under running cold water, drain, pat dry with a clean cloth and then cut into 3–4 cm (1¼–1½ inch) pieces.

For the salad dressing, whisk the mustard, egg yolk, a pinch of salt, the shallot and the vinegars until thick and smooth. Add the stock, then very gradually, and stirring continuously, add the oil. Finish the sauce with the double cream. Toss the asparagus in the dressing and leave to stand for a good hour.

In lukewarm water, carefully pull away the thin transparent membranes covering the brains and wash away any traces of blood. Slice the brains thinly.

Season with salt and pepper, roll in flour, then fry in just-melted butter, for about 1½ minutes each side, until golden brown. Drain on kitchen towel to absorb excess fat.

Arrange the lamb's lettuce decoratively on four plates, drain the asparagus, pile in the middle of the plates, then place 2–3 warm slices of calves' brain beside. If wished, toss the barley in the salad dressing, drain and sprinkle over the salad with the chopped herbs.

Soak the brains in plenty of cold water for several hours

Then carefully remove the thin outer membrane and any small blood clots in warm water

To accompany, try a pungent, dry white wine, such as Sancerre or a
New Zealand Sauvignon Blanc

Cut the brains into 1 cm (½ inch) thick slices, season and coat with flour

Fry on both sides until golden brown, then drain on kitchen towel to absorb excess fat

AUBERGINES WITH BASIL AND SHEEP'S CHEESE
AUBERGINES AU BASILIC ET AU FROMAGE DE BREBIS

Serves 4

2 small aubergines
sea salt
freshly ground black pepper
1 tablespoon flour
4 tablespoons olive oil
1 tablespoon butter
600 g (generous 1¼ lb) ripe
  tomatoes, blanched, skinned, seeded
  and very finely diced
sugar
8–10 basil leaves, shredded
75 g (3 oz) sheep's milk cheese
  (sheep's milk Feta is often available
  from health food stores)
1 sprig of basil

Wash the aubergines and trim off the stalk end, then cut into 0.5 cm (¼ inch) slices lengthways. Season both sides with salt and pepper, then coat with a little flour. Heat 3 tablespoons olive oil until nearly smoking, then quickly sear the aubergines on both sides to lightly colour. Drain on kitchen towel to absorb excess fat.

Melt the butter, add the tomatoes and cook for a few minutes until softened. Season with salt, pepper, and a pinch of sugar, then stir in the shredded basil and the cheese, crumbled. Reserve, off the heat.

Starting with the largest aubergine slices, assemble on a baking sheet, four piles of aubergines, inter-layered with the tomato-cheese mixture, topping with the smallest slices. Sprinkle with the remaining olive oil and bake in the oven, preheated to 220°C/425°F/gas 7, for 4–5 minutes. Serve garnished with a basil sprig.

Cut the aubergines into 0.5 cm (¼ inch) slices lengthways, season, then coat lightly with flour

Sear quickly on both sides in hot olive oil

To accompany, try a red country wine from Corsica (such as Vin de Corse Calvi) or Sardinia (Cannonau di Sardegna)

Sweat the tomatoes in a little butter, season, then mix in the basil and cheese

Assemble four piles of aubergine slices and tomato-cheese mixture, to give each person half an aubergine. Bake in the oven, preheated to 220°C/425°F/ gas 7, for 4–5 minutes

STUFFED COURGETTE FLOWERS
FLEURS DE COURGETTES FARCIES

Serves 4

8 small courgettes with their flowers
 intact

2 tablespoons butter

sea salt

freshly ground white pepper

1 egg yolk

1 teaspoon double cream

For the batter:

250 g (9 oz) flour

5 egg yolks

250 ml (9 fl oz) beer

50 g (2 oz) butter, melted

3 egg whites

sea salt

about 1 kg (2 lbs) clarified butter
 (page 42), or 1 litre (1¾ pints)
 vegetable oil, for frying

For the sauce:

20 g (scant 1 oz) tinned black
 truffles, juice reserved

150 ml (¼ pint) Madeira

300 ml (½ pint) chicken stock (page
 149)

125 ml (4 fl oz) double cream

50 g (2 oz) butter, chilled and flaked

sea salt

First make the batter: make a well in the sifted flour, drop in the egg yolks and mix to blend, then add the beer and melted butter and beat until quite smooth. Leave to rest at room temperature for 30 minutes.

Meanwhile, prepare the courgettes. Carefully cut the flowers off the courgettes, leaving a tiny bit of stem attached to them for easy handling, but gently pulling off the calyx and removing the stigma from inside the flower. Keep aside.

Trim the other end of the courgettes, wash, then dice finely. Melt the butter, add the courgettes and sweat for a few minutes, then season with salt and freshly ground white pepper and leave to cool.

For the sauce, dice the truffles very finely; if wished add a pinch of the chopped truffles to the courgettes, then put the rest in a pan with the truffle juice, Madeira and chicken stock and reduce by nearly half.

Whisk the egg whites for the batter, with a pinch of salt, to the stiff peak stage, then fold gently into the batter. Put the clarified butter or oil into a large wide pan and heat to 180°C/350°F on a fat thermometer.

Mix the courgettes with the egg yolk, double cream and 1 tablespoon batter. Spoon into a piping cone with a medium-sized nozzle. Season the insides of the flowers with a little salt and pepper, then pipe the courgette mixture into the flowers to half fill them. Gently fold the petals over, giving them a little twist to seal.

Whisk the batter again briefly, dip in the flowers, drain them of excess batter, then drop gently into the fat and fry until golden brown on all sides, turning them very carefully with a slotted spoon. Remove, drain well, then put on kitchen towel to absorb excess fat.

Add the double cream to the sauce, whisk in the butter, a few flakes at a time, and adjust the seasoning if necessary.

Pour some sauce on to four warm plates, arrange the courgette flowers on top and serve.

Carefully cut off the courgette flowers, leaving a small piece of stem but removing the calyx and the stigma inside the flowers

Gently open the flowers, season with salt and white pepper, then pipe in the courgette stuffing

*To accompany, try a fine, delicate white wine such as a Spätlese
from the Mosel or an English wine, such as Lamberhurst, Carr
Taylor or Pulham*

Fold over the petals, pressing down
lightly, then twist the ends to seal

Dip the flowers in the batter, drain
and fry in hot fat until golden brown.
Remove from the pan and drain
thoroughly

CHEESE AND SPINACH TART
TARTE AU FROMAGE AT AUX ÉPINARDS

Serves 4
For the pastry:
250 g (9 oz) flour
175 g (6 oz) butter, plus extra for
  greasing
1 egg
sea salt
1 egg yolk, lightly beaten, to glaze
For the filling:
700 g (1½ lbs) spinach, washed and
  trimmed
50 g (2 oz) butter
sea salt
freshly ground black pepper
2 tablespoons double cream
1 teaspoon finely chopped parsley
100 g (3½ oz) Quark cheese
100 g (3½ oz) Emmenthal, grated
For the sauce:
2 large eggs
sea salt
freshly grated nutmeg
125 ml (4 fl oz) double cream
125 ml (4 fl oz) milk
½ teaspoon finely chopped marjoram

Knead together the flour, butter, egg and a pinch of salt to a smooth dough, wrap in cling film and leave in the refrigerator for about 30 minutes.

For the filling, wash the spinach thoroughly in several changes of cold water then drain well in a colander, shaking off all excess moisture. Heat the butter until foaming, then add the spinach. Season with salt and pepper and cook gently, covered, for about 2 minutes.

Meanwhile, beat together all the sauce ingredients, and set aside. Add the cream and parsley to the spinach, then mix in the Quark. Add the Emmenthal, stirring to start the cheese melting. Gradually combine the mixture with the sauce.

Unwrap the pastry dough, halve and roll out thinly on a floured work surface. Line a buttered pie dish with the pastry, and pour in the filling. Roll out the remaining dough and cover the pie. Trim off the surplus pastry around the edges, then press down firmly all the way round to seal. Glaze the top with the beaten egg yolk and prick lightly all over to allow the steam to escape during cooking.

Bake in the oven, preheated to 180°C/350°F/gas 4 for about 30 minutes until golden brown. Serve hot.

Add the spinach to just sizzling butter, season lightly with salt and pepper

Cook gently, covered, for 2 minutes, then mix in the cream, parsley and Quark cheese

*To accompany, try a red or white wine from the Loire valley (Anjou,
Saumur-Champigny), or from Switzerland (Fendant, Dôle)*

Add the Emmenthal to the spinach and
melt, stirring

Stir the spinach mixture into the sauce,
then pour into a greased, pastry-lined
dish. Smooth the filling and cover with
pastry

STUFFED BAKED POTATOES
POMMES DE TERRE FARCIES AU FOUR

Serves 4

*4 medium-sized unblemished potatoes,
of a floury type, i.e. Maris Piper,
Desirée, King Edward (preferably
from the first harvesting of the new
winter crop)*

about 250 g (9 oz) coarse sea salt

*50 g (2 oz) streaky bacon, in one
piece, rind removed, then diced*

1 small shallot, chopped

3 teaspoons finely chopped parsley

1 tablespoon finely chopped chervil

1 tablespoon finely snipped chives

20 g (scant 1 oz) butter

3 tablespoons double cream

*30 g (generous 1 oz) black truffles,
finely chopped, plus extra to garnish,
if wished*

freshly ground white pepper

freshly grated nutmeg

1 egg yolk

2 tablespoons milk

Scrub the potatoes thoroughly, nicking out any eyes if necessary, then make a bed of salt in an ovenproof dish and nestle the potatoes in the salt. Bake in the oven, preheated to 180°C/350°F/gas 4 for about 1 hour until just done. Remove from the dish, cut off the top third of each potato, lengthwise, then scoop out the pulp from the bottom leaving about 0.5 cm (¼ inch) all the way round to hold the potatoes together.

Mash the scooped-out potato until lump free and keep warm – if you want, you can scoop out a little from the lids too.

Fry the bacon gently until the fat starts running, add the shallot and sweat for a couple of minutes, then sprinkle on the chopped herbs and mix.

Beat the butter and cream into the mashed potato, add the bacon mixture, then stir in the chopped truffles. Season well with salt, pepper and nutmeg then stuff into the potato cases. Replace the lids. Whisk the egg yolk and mix together with the milk and use to glaze the lids and potato skins, then return to the oven, at its highest heat, for 5–7 minutes until beautifully golden.

Scoop out the flesh from the bottom of the potatoes, leaving a 'wall' about 0.5 cm (¼ inch) thick all round

Mash the potato, and mix with the butter, cream, the bacon mixture and the truffles

To accompany, try a fruity red Beaujolais Villages or Irouléguy from the Basque country

Divide the filling evenly between the potato cases

Replace the lids, brush the potato skins with the egg yolk and milk glaze, and bake in the oven, at its hottest, until deeply golden

Potato Soup with Cèpes
SOUPE AUX POMMES DE TERRE ET AUX CÈPES

Serves 4
400 g (14 oz) floury potatoes, such as
  King Edward, peeled
sea salt
75 g (3 oz) butter
250 ml (9 fl oz) double cream
about 500 ml (18 fl oz) veal stock
(page 150)
freshly grated nutmeg
freshly ground white pepper
To garnish:
1 medium-sized potato, finely diced
75 g (3 oz) clarified butter (page 42)
65 g (2½ oz) cèpes, cleaned, or 20 g
  (scant 1 oz) dried cèpes, soaked in
  warm water
sea salt
freshly ground white pepper
freshly grated nutmeg
a few chervil leaves

Boil the potatoes in salted water until soft, drain and either mash very thoroughly or push through a coarse sieve – they must be absolutely lump-free. Return the purée to the pan and, while still hot, beat in the butter and cream until smooth. Add the stock gradually, bring the soup to the boil and whisk thoroughly. Season with nutmeg, salt and pepper.

Fry the diced potato in the clarified butter for 3–4 minutes, turning constantly, until crisp and golden brown. Add the sliced cèpes (if using dried cèpes, drain them well, adding the soaking liquid to the soup), stir until cooked, then season with salt, pepper and nutmeg.

Pour the soup into individual soup plates. Drain the potatoes and cèpes, sprinkle over the soup and garnish with chervil leaves.

NOTE: You can replace the cèpes with chanterelles or, extravagant but delicious, use 25 g (1 oz) fresh white truffles. Scrub them well under cold running water and grate them raw on to the soup just before serving.

Mash the boiled potatoes or push through a sieve

While still hot, beat in the butter to make a purée . . .

To accompany, try a fine dry Amontillado or Oloroso sherry

. . . and stir in the cream. Whisk until smooth

Then add the stock and bring the soup to the boil, stirring continuously. Season to taste

POTATO FRITTERS WITH SNAILS
BEIGNETS DE POMMES DE TERRE AUX ESCARGOTS

Serves 4
3 large potatoes, peeled
sea salt
freshly ground black pepper
2–3 tablespoons butter
For the snails:
40 snails, canned
25 g (1 oz) butter
1 teaspoon finely snipped chives
1 teaspoon finely chopped tarragon
1 teaspoon finely chopped parsley
1 teaspoon finely chopped basil
sea salt
freshly ground black pepper
To garnish:
5 mushroom caps wiped with a damp
  cloth, then cut into fine strips

Coarsely grate the potatoes or cut into matchstick strips. Pat dry with kitchen towel and season, then divide into four piles. Melt the butter, add one batch of potato, flatten into a round and fry on both sides until golden brown. Remove from the pan and keep warm, then fry the remaining fritters in the same way, adding a little extra butter if necessary.

Drain the snails and pat dry with kitchen towel, then fry quickly in just sizzling butter to heat through. Add the chopped herbs and season to taste. Serve the potato fritters topped with the snails and sprinkled with the mushroom strips.

NOTE: If you can get hold of fresh snails, they will make a really superb dish. To prepare the snails, tip them into a large pan of boiling water, boil quickly and pour into a sieve. Pull the flesh out of the shells and remove the gut. Mix the snails with about 200 g (7 oz) salt and leave to stand for 1 hour to get rid of the slime. Then wash under cold, running water. Bring about 2 litres (3½ pints) water to the boil with a bunch of stock vegetables, prepared and diced, a few peppercorns, a bay leaf and 250 ml (9 fl oz) white wine. Add the snails and simmer for about 2 hours until tender. They are now ready for the recipe.

Coarsely grate the potatoes or cut into matchstick strips

Pat the potatoes dry with kitchen towel and season with salt and pepper

*To accompany, try a lively young Chablis, or an
Australian Rhine Riesling*

In hot butter, fry four small potato fritters, one at a time, turning them carefully

Cook the snails in butter, add the chopped herbs and season to taste

RÖSTI WITH PASTRY TOPPING
RÖSTI RECOUVERT DE PÂTE

Serves 4
1 large leek, washed
1 tablespoon butter
100 g (3½ oz) chanterelles, stalks trimmed, caps well washed and dried, then chopped
sea salt
freshly ground black pepper
freshly grated nutmeg
1 teaspoon white wine
100 g (3½ fl oz) double cream
2–3 large potatoes, peeled
1 teaspoon finely chopped parsley
1 teaspoon finely chopped chervil
4 tablespoons clarified butter (page 42)
For the topping:
150 g (5 oz) frozen puff pastry, defrosted
flour, for dusting
1 egg yolk, lightly beaten, to glaze
To garnish:
few sprigs of flat parsley

Cut the leek into julienne strips and fry gently in the butter. Add the chanterelles, cook briefly, season with salt, pepper and nutmeg. Add the white wine, stir in the double cream and bring to the boil.

Coarsely grate the potatoes or cut into matchsticks, add the herbs and season with salt and pepper. Melt the clarified butter in a large ovenproof frying pan, sprinkle in the potatoes, pat onto a 'pancake' and fry on both sides until golden brown.

For the topping, roll out the puff pastry on a floured surface as thinly as possible. Carefully drain off any excess fat from the potatoes, leaving them in the pan. Cover with the leek and chanterelle mixture, then with the pastry (it doesn't matter if there are a few folds in this). Glaze with the beaten egg.

Place the pan in the oven, preheated to 220°C/425°F/gas 7 and bake for 8–10 minutes, until puffed up and golden. Serve hot, cut into small slices, garnished with a parsley sprig and accompanied by a mixed salad.

Spread the leek and chanterelle mixture over the fried Rösti in the pan

Carefully spread the thinly rolled puff pastry over the Rösti

*To accompany, try a dry white wine from Savoie, such as Crépy or
Seyssel, or a dry white Swiss wine, such as Forin or Fendant*

Glaze the pastry evenly with the beaten
egg yolk

Bake until golden brown in the oven
preheated to 220°C/425 °F/gas 7 for
8–10 minutes

ONION AND LEEK SOUP WITH CHEESE

SOUPE À L'OIGNON ET AUX POIREAUX ACCOMPAGNÉ DE FROMAGE

Serves 4

3 tablespoons butter

2 large onions, halved, then finely
  sliced

1 leek, washed and finely sliced

2 tablespoons flour

freshly grated nutmeg

500 ml (18 fl oz) dry white wine

500 ml (18 fl oz) warm stock

100 g (3½ oz) Emmenthal cheese
  (more if liked)

freshly ground black pepper

small bunch of parsley, finely chopped

To garnish:

croûtons, made from 2 slices white
  bread, crusts removed

Melt the butter, add the onions and leek and sweat gently without colouring. Sprinkle in the flour, cook briefly until the mixture begins to brown, then season with nutmeg and pour in the wine mixed with the warm stock, stirring continuously.

Bring to the boil, then simmer gently for about 20 minutes, stirring occasionally to prevent the soup from sticking. Dice the cheese, add to the soup and raise the heat slightly to melt. Add a little extra nutmeg, some pepper and the parsley.

Just before serving, garnish with the croûtons.

Gently cook the sliced onions and leek in hot butter without colouring

Add the flour, cook, stirring to brown

To accompany, try a red or white wine from the Côtes de Jura

Pour in the wine and stock, stirring
continuously, and bring the soup to
the boil

Simmer for 20 minutes on a low heat.
Stir occasionally to prevent sticking.
Finally add the diced cheese and cook
until melted

ONION FLAN
FLAN AUX OIGNONS

Serves 4–6
For the pastry:
250 g (9 oz) flour, plus extra for
   dusting
1 egg
175 g (6 oz) butter, plus extra for
   greasing
sea salt
For the filling:
50 g (2 oz) streaky bacon, in one
   piece, rind removed, then diced
175 g (6 oz) onions, finely sliced
4 eggs
200 ml (7 fl oz) milk
400 ml (14 fl oz) double cream
freshly grated nutmeg
freshly ground black pepper
sea salt
1 tablespoon grated Emmenthal cheese
To garnish:
chives, some of them finely snipped

Work all the pastry ingredients together into a smooth dough, either by hand in a large bowl, or whizz together in a food processor until the sides come clean. Wrap in cling film and place in the refrigerator for 30 minutes.

For the filling, blanch the bacon and onions in lightly salted, boiling water for 3–4 minutes – just to mellow the onion flavour and the bacon's saltiness. Meanwhile beat the eggs with the milk and cream, season with nutmeg, pepper and a little salt. Drain the bacon and onions, then wrap in a clean tea towel and squeeze out all the excess moisture.

Unwrap the pastry. The quantities given make enough for two flans. Roll out half the pastry thinly on a floured board and, with the aid of the rolling pin, transfer to a buttered flan or tart tin. Press the pastry to the sides of the tin, then trim off the excess with the rolling pin. Knead the trimmings into the unused pastry, wrap in cling film and chill or freeze (it will keep up to a week in the refrigerator in a sealed bag).

Spread the bacon and onions evenly in the tin, sprinkle with the cheese and pour in the eggs, milk and cream, having first whisked them quickly again. Bake in the oven, preheated to 200°C/400°F/gas 6 for 40 minutes. To check that the flan is cooked: prick the centre with a wooden cocktail stick. It should come out dry.

To serve, cut the flan into portions and garnish with chives, some whole, some finely snipped.

Place the thinly rolled pastry in a buttered tin and press evenly all the way round

Trim off the excess pastry, running the rolling pin over the tin

To accompany, try a white wine from Alsace, such as Pinot Blanc,
Pinot Gris or Riesling

Spread the blanched bacon and onions evenly in the tin and sprinkle with the cheese

Pour on the beaten eggs, milk and cream. Bake in the oven, preheated to 200°C/400°F/gas 6, for 40 minutes until golden brown

DESSERTS

'FRUIT IS WITH US ALMOST THE entire year around, and when it appears on the table it should reflect the season, be it an autumn compôte, fruit in brandy for winter, or fruit with the freshness of spring or the ripeness of summer. Nowadays we take it for granted that every tropical fruit can be flown in. Yet nothing can beat the produce of your own garden. I remember a dish my grandmother used to make. She picked anything in the garden which had not fully ripened, cut it into small pieces, sautéd it in butter like fried potatoes and sprinkled sugar over it. A poem.' These are Bocuse's feelings about fruit and this chapter shows how fruit of every kind, treated in the Bocuse manner, can form the most delicious of desserts.

Fruit has long played a double role in history – growing by the wayside, it was nature's bounty, and food for the poor. Cultivated in extravagantly built glasshouses by the rich, or brought from far-off lands by galleon, it was a luxury, a food fit for kings and queens. By the 1600s, many of Europe's monarchs had constructed their own orangeries, though none so palatial as Louis XIV's at Versailles, where 1200 orange trees stood proudly in their silver tubs.

For painters of the Dutch school, fruit of all sorts came to life on their canvasses. Bunches of grapes, black and white; soft-bloomed, blushing peaches; pomegranates, darkly red and succulent – they almost beg to be plucked off the wall and eaten.

Perhaps Eve should have followed Grandmère Bocuse's example, and cooked her quince instead of biting into the sourness of that fruit raw (although the ancients apparently enjoyed its astringency). Few today, however, would argue that, cooked, it is one of the heavenly fruits. And it is in the cooking that fruit displays its versatility. From the necessity of preservation came the myriad recipes for jams, jellies, fruit cheese, sweet pastes, green nuts and lemons pickled in brine, sweet fruits and oranges preserved in cognac, liqueurs made from the fruits themselves. From preserves it was but one step to dishes eaten freshly made, but dishes that could give variety when there was a glut – pies and crumbles, fools and mousses, blancmanges and jellies, ice creams and sorbets. For the delicacies of summer, with but a short season, the treatments were fresh and simple: strawberries and raspberries with newly made cream, peaches with wine, blackberries straight off the bush with a sprinkling of sugar.

From all these evolved a huge repetoire of wonderful desserts, which could both reflect the season and the sense of the occasion. The dessert need not always be grand but 'a beautiful dessert should form the crowning glory to every meal. It is a bit like the Grand Finale of an opera. The Finale is very important because this is what people remember most clearly. I personally am especially fond of crêpes, waffles and hot rice and semolina puddings, like my mother and grandmother used to make.'

Crêpes, from the flamboyant Suzette, to the traditional Shrove Tuesday lemon pancakes, are obligingly adaptable. The fresh sharpness of the latter is delicious, but also symbolic of the event. The richness that Bocuse endows on crêpes – stuffed with marinated fruits, or a sweet hazelnut sauce – gives them not only grandeur, but a seasonal touch too.

For in fruit, above all, Bocuse listens to the seasons: 'I am of the old-fashioned opinion that you should eat strawberries in summer and not in December.' So, in summer he will use strawberries plentifully in a chilled buttermilk soup, sparingly at the end of their time to garnish a rich coffee ice. The first apricots are refreshingly partnered with light yoghurt creams, and as they progress through the season he is quite happy to make a compôte, enriched with curd-cheese dumplings.

With autumn's arrival, he embraces the apple and the pear. Discimination in variety is important. He is not above serving apple fritters, crisply coated and scented with cinnamon, but the choice of the apple is vital. It must have a crunch, and a sharp-sweet flavour. Pears too are carefully chosen – not for the French, Conference pears and nothing else, which is understandable for the country that, in the seventeenth century, was the country for pears. Three hundred varieties were grown, many of them around Paris. Despite the palace he built for his oranges, Louis XIV rarely displayed much interest in them, beyond a passing question as to their health. But for the pear he had a passion. To satiate that passion, his gardener-in-chief grew 25 varieties on the walls of Versailles. Among them was the parent of the pear favoured by Bocuse: Williams' Bon Chrétien. The Bon Chrétien (so-called in honour of St François de Paul, whose nickname it was) had been known since the 1400s: in Louis' inventory it was listed as the Bon Chrétien *d'hiver*. Only in 1770, in England, did the Williams' Bon Chrétien (or Bartlett pear) come into being, at the hands of one John Stair. Much as Stilton (one of the pear's natural soulmates) gained its name by first being noticed in the town of that name, so the Williams' pear remembers its distributors – Mr Williams in Great Britain, Mr Bartlett in the USA – rather than the schoolmaster who cherished his orchard so fruitfully. Still, his pear, along with the newer Doyenne de Comice (born Angers, 1850) is considered by gourmets to be one of the finest.

And when its season is over, Bocuse turns his attention to the orange – simply grilled, but on a bed of featherlight meringue-cream. For a really rich *pièce-de-resistance* on the winter table, though, Bocuse produces elegant diamonds of bitter chocolate – filled with the sweetness of puréed chestnuts, gilded with a sauce of that even sweeter winter nut – the hazel.

APRICOT AND YOGHURT CREAMS
CRÈMES À L'ABRICOT ET AU YAOURT

Serves 4
400 g (14 oz) ripe apricots
about 75 g (3 oz) sugar
lemon juice
150 g (5 oz) strawberries, hulled
300 g (11 oz) Quark cheese,
  fromage frais, or skimmed milk
  curd cheese
100 ml (3½ fl oz) yoghurt
125 ml (4 fl oz) double cream

To decorate:
4 strawberries
few slices of apricot

Scald the apricots in boiling water, transfer to a bowl of cold water and rub off the skins. Quarter the fruit, discarding the stones, and cut into bite-sized pieces, then put in a bowl with 40 g (1½ oz) sugar and a little lemon juice, and leave to marinate.

Wash and slice the strawberries, putting them in a separate bowl to marinate in a few drops of lemon juice and 1 teaspoon sugar.

Squeeze the Quark cheese in a muslin until quite dry, then beat with the yoghurt and the remaining sugar until creamy. (Skimmed milk curd cheese is dryer than Quark or *fromage frais* and will not need squeezing.) Whip the cream until stiff and gently fold in, then fold in the apricots and their juice.

Divide the mixture between four shallow dishes, place a strawberry in the centre of each and top with a few apricot slices and the marinated strawberries.

Squeeze the Quark cheese in a clean cloth to get rid of excess moisture

Beat the Quark, yoghurt and sugar until creamy. Whip the cream until stiff and fold in

To accompany, try a French Muscat Vin Doux Naturel, such as
Muscat de Beaumes de Venise or Muscat de Lunel

Add the marinated apricots . . .

. . . and fold gently. The creams are
now ready to serve, garnished with
apricots and strawberries

CURD CHEESE DUMPLINGS WITH APRICOT COMPÔTE
BOULETTES DE FROMAGE BLANC À LA COMPÔTE D'ABRICOTS

Serves 4

700 g (1½ lbs) Quark, or other
    low-fat curd cheese

50 g (2 oz) butter, softened

3 eggs

sea salt

4 tablespoons sugar

140 g (4½ oz) white bread, grated

1 lemon, scrubbed thoroughly

For the apricot compote:

350 g (12 oz) ripe apricots

500 ml (18 fl oz) water

75 g (3 oz) sugar

5 cm (2 inch) cinnamon stick

1 clove

juice of ½ lemon

rind of ½ lemon, lemon scrubbed well
    first, then thinly peeled and all pith
    removed

For the buttered breadcrumbs:

100 g (3½ oz) butter

65 g (2½ oz) sugar

75 g (3 oz) breadcrumbs

1 teaspoon ground cinnamon

To decorate:

mint leaves

To make the apricot compote, wash, halve and stone the apricots. Bring all the other compote ingredients to the boil in a saucepan, add the apricots and cook over a low heat for about 20 minutes until tender.

For the dumplings, squeeze the Quark, a little at a time, in muslin, to remove all excess moisture. Beat in the softened butter, mixing well, then add the eggs, a pinch of salt, the sugar and grated white bread, and beat thoroughly. Leave to stand for about 30 minutes.

To grate the lemon, wrap a piece of greaseproof paper around the grater. Rub the lemon on the paper, then carefully remove the paper and scrape off the zest with the back of a knife. Squeeze the lemon, then stir the grated zest and juice into the dumpling mixture and leave to stand for 20 minutes.

Stir the mixture again, then shape into small dumplings and drop gently into a pan of simmering salted water. Cook for 15–20 minutes.

To make the buttered breadcrumbs, melt the butter in a frying pan, add the sugar and dissolve. Stir in the breadcrumbs and cinnamon, brown for a few minutes and then keep to one side.

Drain the dumplings well, coat in the buttered breadcrumbs and arrange on individual plates. Remove the lemon rind, cinnamon stick and clove from the compote. Place a few apricot halves on each plate beside the dumplings, pour over a little juice and decorate with mint leaves.

Rub the lemon on a grater wrapped in greaseproof paper, remove the paper and carefully scrape off the zest

Shape the dumpling mixture, a little at a time, into small dumplings

To accompany, try a dry apricot eau-de-vie *from Alsace or Hungary*

Add to simmering salted water, cook for 15–20 minutes and then drain well

Coat the dumplings in the buttered breadcrumbs and serve with the apricot compote

APPLE FRITTERS
BEIGNETS DE POMMES

Serves 4

*450 g (1 lb) sharp-flavoured dessert
apples, i.e. Sturmer, Pippins, or a
firm cooker such as Newton Wonder
or Lord Denby*

juice of 1 lemon

½ tablespoon rum

40 g (1½ oz) sugar

*250 g (9 oz) clarified butter (page
42)*

cinnamon sugar

For the batter:

125 g (4 oz) flour

sea salt

2 teaspoons sugar

125 ml (4 fl oz) beer

1 egg yolk

25 g (1 oz) butter, melted

1 egg white

For the rum cream:

½ tablespoon sugar

2 tablespoons rum

150 ml (¼ pint) double cream

To make the batter, sift the flour, add a pinch of salt, the sugar and then pour in the beer gradually, stirring constantly until smooth. Beat in the egg yolk and melted butter. Whisk the egg white until stiff, then fold in gently. Leave to rest in a warm place for 30 minutes.

Core the apples, then slice into 1 cm (about ½ inch) rings, sprinkling with lemon juice to prevent discoloration. Marinate the apples in the rum, sugar and, if wished, a pinch of cinnamon.

Melt the clarified butter in a wide pan, and heat to 180°C/350°F on a fat thermometer. Dip the apple rings in the batter, shaking off excess, then drop, a few at a time, into the pan. Cook for a minute or so, until the underside is golden, then turn carefully to colour and crisp the second side. Drain on kitchen towel to absorb excess fat, then toss in cinnamon sugar.

For the rum cream, lightly stir the sugar and rum into the softly whipped cream. Serve the fritters hot with a couple of spoonfuls of cream beside them.

Dip the apple rings into the beer batter

Lift out with the handle of a fork or spoon to drain off excess batter, then drop into the hot fat

To accompany, try a tot of rum, or a glass of Calvados

Once golden underneath, turn and cook the second side

Drain the fritters on kitchen towel to absorb excess fat, then toss in a mixture of ground cinnamon and sugar

GRILLED ORANGES
ORANGES GRILLÉES

Serves 4

6 large unblemished oranges

3 tablespoons orange liqueur, i.e.
Cointreau, Curaçao, Grand Marnier

40 g (1 ½ oz) icing sugar

2 egg yolks

25 g (1 oz) sugar

40 g (1 ½ oz) Quark, or other low-fat
skimmed milk cheese

100 ml (3 ½ fl oz) double cream,
whipped

2 egg whites

soft light brown sugar

Using a lemon zester, pare away eight strips of peel from one orange, top to bottom, at even intervals. Halve the orange lengthwise, then cut each half into fine slices. Reserve.

Peel the other oranges, removing all the pith, then divide into segments and, over a bowl to catch the juices, carefully peel off the inner skin from each segment. Squeeze the inner skins of all juice into the bowl. Add half the orange liqueur, a touch of icing sugar, then place the orange segments in a shallow dish and pour over the juice to marinate.

Beat the egg yolks with the granulated and icing sugars until frothy and increased in volume. Whisk in the Quark and the whipped cream, then beat the egg whites to the stiff peak stage and fold gently in. Flavour with the rest of the orange liqueur.

Divide the marinating segments between four heatproof plates, pile on the meringue-cream mixture and put under a hot grill to brown – but watch constantly so they don't burn. Quickly make a circle around the edge of each plate with the half-slices of orange, sprinkle with a little brown sugar and serve immediately.

Pare away eight strips of peel, at even intervals, all round one orange, using lemon zester from top to bottom

Peel the other oranges, removing all the pith

*Follow with coffee served with a glass of the same liqueur as that
used to make the dessert*

Segment the oranges then, over a bowl
to catch the juices, skin the segments

Marinate the segments in the orange
juice, half the liqueur and a little icing
sugar

WILLIAM'S PEAR CHARLOTTE
CHARLOTTE AUX POIRES WILLIAMS

Serves 5

1 kg (2 lbs) ripe William's pears

juice of 2½ lemons

*1 litre (1¾ pints) light sugar syrup
(made from 1 litre (1¾ pints) water
and 300 g (11 oz) sugar, simmered
until the sugar has completely
dissolved)*

*zest of 1 lemon (lemon should be well
washed first)*

1 mint leaf

125 ml (4 fl oz) white wine

125 ml (4 fl oz) dry sparkling wine

2 leaves of gelatine

4 tablespoons pear brandy

2 egg whites

25 g (1 oz) sugar

For the blackcurrant sauce:

*225 g (8 oz) blackcurrants, off the
stalk, rinsed and lightly cooked*

*3 tablespoons sugar, depending on the
sweetness of the currants*

2 tablespoons Crème de Cassis

To decorate:

blackcurrants

mint leaves

Peel, halve and core the pears, dropping them into a bowl of cold water, acidulated with the juice of 1 lemon, to prevent discoloration. In a saucepan, bring to the boil the sugar syrup, juice of 1 lemon, the lemon zest and mint with two-thirds of the white and sparkling wines. Add five pear halves and poach for 5–6 minutes.

Chop the remaining pears and boil with the rest of the lemon juice, sparkling and white wines until very soft and mushy. Put the gelatine leaves in cold water to soak and soften.

Remove the poached pear halves from the juice and leave to cool. Then cut, lengthways, into thin slices and use to line five individual moulds, overlapping the slices.

Lightly wash the other pears, then press through a coarse sieve to give about 250 g (9 oz) purée. Stir in the pear brandy. Squeeze out the gelatine leaves and stir into the pear purée until dissolved, then stand in iced water to cool. Once the purée is starting to set, whisk the egg whites until stiff, gradually adding the sugar, then fold into the pear purée. Spoon into the individual moulds and chill for about 2 hours.

To make the sauce, mix the blackcurrants with the sugar and Crème de Cassis and strain through a sieve. If the sauce is too thick you can thin it with a little blackcurrant juice or water.

Pour the sauce on to individual serving plates, turn the charlottes carefully out of the moulds to sit in a pool of sauce, and decorate with a few blackcurrants and mint leaves.

Overlap the thinly sliced pears to line individual moulds

Cool the pear purée by stirring continuously over iced water

*To accompany, try a fine Asti Spumante (for example, that of
Fontanafredda or Contratto), or and Alsace* eau-de-vie de poire

Fold the whisked egg white carefully
into the pear purée as it begins to set

Spoon the mousse into the pear-lined
moulds and chill for about 2 hours in
the refrigerator

Rum Pudding with Pears in Red Wine

ENTREMET AU RHUM ACCOMPAGNÉ DE POIRES AU VIN ROUGE

Serves 4

For the pears in red wine:

½ vanilla pod

7.5–10 cm (3–4 inch) cinnamon
  stick

1 clove

250 ml (9 fl oz) red wine

75 g (3 oz) sugar

juice of ½ lemon

juice of ½ orange

2 large ripe pears (such as William's
  or Doyenné)

For the Rum Pudding:

125 g (4 oz) butter, softened, plus
  extra for greasing

75 g (3 oz) sugar

2 egg yolks

40 g (1½ oz) ground hazelnuts,
  lightly roasted

25 g (1 oz) grated chocolate

pinch of baking powder

pinch of ground cinnamon

75 g (3 oz) flour

1 tablespoon rum

3 egg whites

1 tablespoon home-made dried
  breadcrumbs

To decorate:

lemon balm or mint leaves

icing sugar

To cook the pears, place the first seven ingredients, except the pears, in a pan, and bring to the boil.

Peel and halve the pears, then core, using a ball cutter. Cut off the stalks, scoop out the tough fibres with an apple corer. Add the pears to the boiling wine, making sure they are completely immersed. Take the pan off the heat and leave to stand for about 6 hours.

To make the rum pudding, beat the butter with half the sugar until light and fluffy. Lightly whisk the egg yolks, then add gradually to the butter, beating briskly. Mix together the hazelnuts, chocolate, baking powder, ground cinnamon and flour; fold into the butter and egg mixture, together with the rum.

Whisk the egg whites until stiff, sprinkling in the remaining sugar and then gently fold the whites into the pudding. Lightly butter four individual moulds and sprinkle with the breadcrumbs, then spoon the pudding into the moulds. Stand the moulds in a roasting pan in 2.5 cm (1 inch) water and bake in the oven, preheated to 180°C/350°F/gas 4, for 18–20 minutes.

Remove the pears from the wine, dry with kitchen towel and place cut side down on a flat surface. Holding the pears at the stalk end, cut lengthways into slices, leaving the end uncut. Transfer to individual plates. Press down lightly on the pears and surround with the red wine.

Carefully unmould the rum puddings on to the plates, beside the pears. Decorate with lemon balm or mint leaves and a sprinkling of icing sugar.

Core the peeled pear halves using a ball cutter

Drain the pears after marinating in the red wine

To accompany, try a tot of rum, or a glass of Vintage Character port

Cut lengthways into slices, leaving the stalk end uncut

Press down on the pears to fan out the slices

Cold Buttermilk Fruit Soup
SOUPE FROIDE AU BABEURRE ET AUX FRUITS

Serves 4
1 egg yolk
1 tablespoon vinegar
sea salt
100 ml (3½ fl oz) light vegetable oil,
i.e. peanut or sunflower
250 g (9 oz) strawberries, washed and
hulled
100 ml (3½ fl oz) sparkling wine
125 ml (4 fl oz) double cream
300 ml (½ pint) buttermilk
lemon juice
To decorate
strawberry slices
a few sprigs of lemon balm, optional

Whisk the egg yolk with the vinegar and a pinch of salt until creamy, gradually adding the oil, a little at a time, to make a mayonnaise.

Cut up half the strawberries, place in a liquidiser and add the wine. Blend quickly, gradually adding the cream and buttermilk, blending after each addition. Whisk the strawberry mixture into the mayonnaise and sharpen to taste with lemon juice, then chill in refrigerator for several hours.

Dice the remaining strawberries, divide between four chilled soup plates, and pour in the soup. Decorate with a few slices of strawberry and, if wished, a sprig or two of lemon balm. An excellent summer starter.

Whisk the egg yolk, vinegar and salt until creamy, gradually adding the oil

Place the chopped strawberries and the wine in a liquidiser and blend

To accompany, try a Hungarian Tokay Aszu or an Austrian Auslese

Gradually add the cream and buttermilk, blending each time

Whisk the strawberry mixture into the mayonnaise and flavour to taste with lemon juice

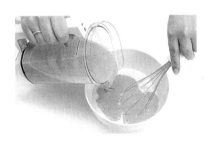

STUFFED HAZELNUT CRÊPES
CRÊPES FARCIES AUX NOISETTES

Serves 4
65 g (2½ oz) flour
6 tablespoons milk
100 ml (3½ fl oz) double cream
3 eggs
sea salt
pith from ½ vanilla pod (see Note)
grated zest of ½ lemon, lemon
   thoroughly washed first
1 tablespoon clarified butter (page
   42), browned

For the filling:
2 egg yolks
1 tablespoon icing sugar
40 g (1½ oz) hazelnuts or walnuts,
   grated (or ground in a spice grinder)
2 egg whites
2 tablespoons sugar

For the pear sauce:
3 egg yolks
75 g (3 oz) sugar
8 tablespoons white wine
8 tablespoons dry sparkling wine
4 tablespoons pear brandy

To decorate:
1 pear
1 tablespoon butter
sugar
icing sugar

Beat together the flour, milk, cream, eggs, a pinch of salt, vanilla and grated lemon zest. Stir in the browned butter and leave the batter to stand for at least 15 minutes.

To make the filling, whisk the egg yolks and icing sugar until frothy, then stir in the nuts. Whisk the egg whites until stiff, slowly adding the sugar. Gently fold the whites, a little at a time, into the nut mixture.

For the sauce, whisk the egg yolks, sugar, white and sparkling wines in a bain-marie until the mixture thickens. Add the pear brandy, whisk well once more and keep hot.

Brush a non-stick frying pan with melted butter, pour in a ladleful or so of batter, swirl it round to coat the pan, and quickly fry thin pancakes. Place a little of the hazelnut filling on each, and fold the pancakes in half. Place the pancakes, in pairs, slightly overlapping, on an ovenproof plate or buttered baking sheet and pour a little sauce over each pair.

Brown in the oven, preheated to 180°C/350°F/gas 4, for about 5 minutes. Meanwhile peel, quarter, core and thinly slice the pear. Fry quickly in hot butter and sugar to taste. Transfer the pancakes to individual plates, decorate with the fried pears and a sprinkling of icing sugar and serve with the rest of the hot pear sauce.

NOTE: Split the vanilla pod lengthways and scrape out the soft inner lining.

Brush a frying pan with butter and quickly fry thin pancakes

Spread the hazelnut filling on the pancakes

To accompany, try a sweet Sauternes or Monbazillac, or an Alsace
eau-de-vie de poire

Fold the pancakes in half

Place in pairs, overlapping, on a
buttered baking sheet or ovenproof
plate and pour on a little pear sauce.
Brown at 180°C/350°F/gas 4 for about
5 minutes

CRÊPES BOCUSE
CRÊPES BOCUSE

Serves 4

40 g (1½ oz) butter, plus extra for
  frying
25 g (1 oz) flour
25 g (1 oz) cornflour
sea salt
250 ml (9 fl oz) milk
3 egg yolks
3 egg whites
25 g (1 oz) sugar

For the orange sauce:

segments from 2 oranges, skinned
5 tablespoons orange liqueur, i.e.
  Cointreau, Curaçao, or Grand
  Marnier
250 g (9 oz) raspberries, picked over
  and stalks removed
50 g (2 oz) butter
75 g (3 oz) sugar
400 ml (14 fl oz) orange juice
zest of 1 orange, cut into julienne
  strips
zest of 1 lemon, cut into julienne
  strips (both fruits well washed first)
1 egg yolk

To decorate:

few pistachio nuts, chopped
icing sugar

Melt the butter, sprinkle in the flour, cornflour and a pinch of salt and stir thoroughly to make a smooth roux. Add the milk gradually, stirring constantly to ensure a lump-free mixture and bring to the boil. Transfer the batter to a mixing bowl and beat in the egg yolks, one at a time. Whisk the egg whites until stiff, slowly adding the sugar, then gently fold the whites, a little at a time, into the batter.

To make the sauce, place the orange segments in a shallow dish with 2 tablespoons orange liqueur, stir in the raspberries, and leave to marinate.

Melt the butter, add the sugar and stir until you have a golden-brown caramel, about 5 minutes. Add the orange juice, orange and lemon zests, stir thoroughly and bring to the boil. Meanwhile, melt a small knob of butter in a frying pan and, when just sizzling, quickly fry eight small pancakes, two or three at a time, until golden on both sides. Keep them hot on a plate over a pan of simmering water.

Finish the sauce by beating the egg yolk with the remaining orange liqueur, add to the pan and stir until lightly thickened. Add the marinated fruit, and its juice, and quickly heat through.

Place a pancake on each of four plates, and cover with fruit. Top the fruit with a second pancake and pour over a little orange sauce. Sprinkle with the chopped pistachios and icing sugar and serve immediately.

Whisk the milk into the flour and butter mixture until smooth and bring to the boil

Transfer the batter to a mixing bowl, and gradually whisk in the egg yolks

*Follow with coffee served with a glass of the same liqueur as that
used to make the dessert*

Whisk the egg whites with the sugar
until stiff and fold the whites into the
batter

In the hot butter fry, in batches, eight
small, golden-brown pancakes. Keep
hot

COFFEE ICE CREAM
GLACE AU CAFÉ

Serves 10

225 g (8 oz) sugar

5 tablespoons water

10 egg yolks

4 tablespoons coffee, preferably made with mocha coffee

100 ml (3½ fl oz) rum

600 ml (1 pint) double cream, whipped

For the sauce:

3 egg yolks

65 g (2½ oz) icing sugar

150 g (5 oz) mascarpone

2 teaspoons rum

1 tablespoon lemon juice

150 ml (¼ pint) whipping cream, lightly whipped

To decorate:

strawberries, thinly sliced

lemon balm leaves

Measure out 175 g (6 oz) sugar, pour into a pan, add the water, stir and bring to the boil. Boil until thick and syrupy but don't let it colour: a spoon dipped in and lifted up should see the sugar running off in thin threads.

Whisk the egg yolks with the remaining sugar until frothy and increased in volume, then slowly add the syrup, stirring constantly. Keep stirring until the mixture has cooled.

And the coffee and rum, then fold in the whipped cream, blending thoroughly.

Spoon into a freezer-proof container and freeze for 2–3 hours until just frozen all the way through. For the sauce, whisk the egg yolks with the sugar until frothy, then stir in the mascarpone, rum and lemon juice. Lastly, fold in the lightly whipped cream.

Make a pool of sauce on chilled individual plates. To unmould the ice cream, dip the bottom in hot water briefly, turn on to a plate, and cut into 2 cm (¾ inch) slices, dipping the knife into hot water between cutting each slice. Put two slices on each plate and decorate with strawberries and a lemon balm leaf on each slice.

When cooked, the sugar syrup should run off the spoon in fine threads

Slowly add the syrup to the egg yolk-sugar mixture, whisking constantly

Follow with coffee and cognac

Stir constantly until cool, then mix in the coffee and rum

Fold in the whipped cream, then spoon into a freezer-proof container and freeze for 2–3 hours

CHOCOLATE LEAVES WITH CHESTNUT PURÉE AND HAZELNUT SAUCE
FEUILLES DE CHOCOLAT À LA PURÉE DE MARRONS SAUCE AUX NOISETTES

Serves 4

*200 g (7 oz) dark cooking chocolate,
  i.e.* chocolat menier

For the purée:

*400 g (14 oz) fresh chestnuts
2 litres (3¹/₂ pints) water
40 g (1¹/₂ oz) sugar
sea salt
500 ml (18 fl oz) double cream
2 tablespoons cherry brandy
2 egg whites
3 tablespoons whipping cream, lightly
  whipped*

For the sauce:

*125 ml (4 fl oz) milk
200 g (7 oz) hazelnut nougat
1 tablespoon hazelnut liqueur (crème
  de nois)
6 tablespoons whipping cream, lightly
  whipped*

To decorate:

icing sugar

Break up the chocolate and melt in a bowl over a pan of simmering water. Once completely melted, remove it from the heat and stir constantly until barely tepid to the touch, a temperature of 32°C/90°F. Pour on to a board covered with greaseproof paper, smoothing it out thinly and evenly with a palette knife, and leave briefly in a cool place, not the refrigerator.

Once firm but not rock hard, cut into diamonds 6 × 5 cm (2¾ × 2 inches). Separate them slightly and leave to cool and harden further.

With a very sharp pointed knife, make a slit on the flat side of each chestnut (hold the nuts in a towel in the palm of the hand to avoid accidents). Put in a large pan with the water, 25 g (1 oz) sugar and a pinch of salt and cook until very tender, 40 minutes–1 hour depending on the age of the nuts. Remove a few at a time, and peel, then rub off the inner soft brown skin. Keep the water at a bare simmer while peeling the nuts as, once they cool, it's much harder to remove the shells. Once peeled, chop the nuts in half, then heat briefly with the double cream. Stir in the cherry brandy then either purée in a food processor or push through a coarse sieve. Leave to cool.

Whisk the egg whites until stiff, trickling in the rest of the sugar towards the end of the whisking. Fold into the chestnut purée, together with the whipped cream, then spoon into a piping bag with a star-shaped nozzle and chill very lightly.

For the sauce, heat the milk, add the nougat and cook gently until the nougat has quite dissolved, stirring from time to time. Flavour with the *crème de nois*, then fold in the whipped cream.

Pipe some chestnut purée on to eight of the chocolate diamonds, cover each lightly with another piece of chocolate and again pipe on some purée. Make a little pool of hazelnut sauce on four plates, arrange two chocolate parcels on each and sprinkle with a little icing sugar.

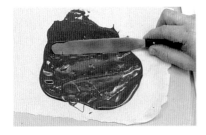

Spread the melted chocolate thinly and evenly on greaseproof paper

Cut the chocolate once firm, but not too hard, into 6×5 cm (2¾×2 inch) diamonds. Separate slightly

Follow with coffee and a rich Spanish brandy

Pipe some chestnut purée on to the chocolate, cover with another diamond, and pipe on more purée

Build up as many or as few chocolate layers as you like (up to a maximum of four layers). Serve on the hazelnut sauce as shown

PASTRIES

ONE OF THE MOST MEMORABLE THINGS on a first journey through France is perhaps the sight of the pâtisseries. Every village, however tiny, seems to have at least one, sometimes two. The windows are crammed. Enormous gleaming *tartes aux pommes* are surrounded by miniature tartlets, filled with delicious confectioner's custard, covered with ultra fine slices of strawberry, or whole raspberries, or seedless grapes, packed tightly together. Crisp choux pastry makes elegantly long éclairs, dripping with chocolate, or, more spectacularly, the pastry is puffed into small rounds, layered into teetering pyramids and brushed with a thin brittle caramel glaze. Savarins bulge with fruits and almost reek of alcohol, and the *petits fours* melt in the mouth as you look at them.

No wonder then that the French housewife is content to buy her celebratory cakes from the pâttissier, sure in the knowledge that the pastry will always be perfectly crisp, the sponges moist, the fillings plentiful. She need make no apologies – either for the quality or the fact that the professional has made them. To her, it is most logical that it should be so. Pâtisserie-making is a skilled art: when the French want a special cake, they go to the specialist.

That does not mean the housewife will not bake at home. But she will concentrate on the flans and cakes 'best . . . baked in the home, not confectioners and pastry-chefs in restaurants. A simple apple flan in autumn, a gâteau with soft fruit when they are ripe in summer, or a chocolate cake – what could be better than that!' She will make upside-down pear tarts; clafoutis – the wonderful batter cake which rises to hide a layer of juicy black cherries; small tarts of fruits of the garden – rhubarb, black- and redcurrants, greengages or the golden Mirabelle plum. Prunes soaked in Armagnac will be bought – but put into puff pastry cases. Plums will have puff pastry over and under them to make a *jalousie,* so-called from the slits in the top, resembling a venetian blind.

Cheesecakes are popular in the Alsace region, nut cakes in Limousin – reflecting, as one would expect, abundant use of the local produce, a principle endorsed by Bocuse: 'My personal favourites are bilberries, raspberries and wild strawberries,' and he goes to the hedgerow, too, for elderberries, to make a wonderful sauce for the lightest of batch buns. A glut of plums is transformed into glowing, Burgundy-coloured sorbets – to contrast in temperature and texture with hot poppy cakes, while autumn's nuts give crunchy buns to be richly coated with melted dark chocolate.

We may not have the pâtisserie tradition of the French, but we do have a great tradition of home-baking; sponge cakes, fruit cakes, gingerbreads, and the childhood favourite, chocolate cake. A foundation so good should be treasured, though maybe we could also take a lesson from Bocuse and combine the simple with the rich, the unusual with the traditional, to give a new look to ancient ideas.

But neither should we forget the old themes – for they are the heritage of cooking: 'Carmen always remains Carmen, Wagner too, and Beethoven's 5th likewise. Although there has been new music, we still hear the old music time and again. And I believe it's rather like that with cookery too.' Such modesty can only come from a man who is master of his art.

Gâteau Saint Honoré

Serves 8-10

*125 g (4 oz) frozen puff pastry,
  defrosted*

butter, for greasing

icing sugar, for dusting

For the choux pastry:

250 ml (9 fl oz) water

100 g (3½ oz) butter

25 g (1 oz) sugar

pinch of salt

125 g (4 oz) flour

3 eggs, beaten

For the confectioner's custard:

250 ml (9 fl oz) milk

1 vanilla pod, cut in half lengthways

3 eggs, separated

125 g (4 oz) caster sugar

20 g (scant 1 oz) cornflour

2 gelatine leaves

First, roll the puff pastry into a round of 25 cm (10 inches) diameter and about 0.5 cm (¼ inch) thick, and place on a buttered baking sheet. Prick this base with a fork and keep to one side.

Make the choux pastry. In a saucepan, bring the water, together with the butter, sugar and salt, to the boil. Remove from the heat and stir in the flour. Place the pan over a moderate heat for 2-3 minutes, stirring until the mixture comes cleanly away from the sides of the pan. Remove the pan from the heat and add the eggs, a little at a time.

Transfer the choux pastry into a piping bag fitted with a 2.5 cm (1 inch) nozzle and pipe on to the round of puff pastry. Then pipe 16 small rounds of pastry on to a separate buttered baking sheet.

Place both baking sheets in an oven preheated to 240°C/450°F/gas 8. Bake for 15 minutes, then reduce the heat to 220°C/400°F/gas 6. Bake the small choux for a further 5 minutes, then remove from the oven, leaving the puff pastry for another 5 minutes.

While the pastry is baking, prepare the confectioner's custard. Bring the milk to the boil with the vanilla pod. In a basin, whisk the egg yolks with the sugar until thick and quite pale in colour. Add the cornflour, then pour the boiling milk into the eggs, beating continuously. Return the mixture to the pan, remove the vanilla pod, then bring gently back to the boil, continuing to beat vigorously, until nicely thickened. Keep warm over a bain-marie. In a small basin, put the gelatine leaves to soak in a little water.

Pierce the small choux with a knife. Fill a piping bag with some of the confectioner's custard, and fill each small choux with about one third of the custard. Return any unused custard to the pan, then add the gelatine, squeezed dry of excess water, and stir gently to dissolve. Remove from the heat. Whisk the egg whites until stiff peaks form, then fold gently into the custard. Pipe this over the cake base.

Arrange the small choux in a ring around the edge of the cake, leave to cool and then chill. Dust with icing sugar before serving.

For the choux pastry, remove the pan from the heat once the water and butter mixture has boiled, then add the eggs a little at a time, beating very vigorously

Pipe the mixture on to the round of puff pastry, starting with a ring round the edge and working in a spiral toward the centre

To accompany, serve coffee with a glass of cognac, armagnac or calvados if wished.

On removing the small choux from the oven, pierce each one with a sharp knife tip, then fill with confectioner's custard

Pipe confectioner's custard over the base of the cake

FRENCH APPLE TARTS WITH RUM CREAM
TARTELETTES AUX POMMES À LA CRÈME AU RHUM

Serves 4
400 g (14 oz) flaky pastry
flour for dusting
butter for greasing
2 teaspoons ground hazelnuts
35 g (scant 1½ oz) marzipan
4 apples (large Cox's or Reinette's)
1–2 tablespoons apricot jam

For the rum cream:
200 ml (7 fl oz) double cream
1 tablespoon sugar
4 tablespoons rum

To decorate:
1–2 tablespoons sugar crystals

On a floured surface, roll out the pastry thinly, then use a small saucepan lid to cut out four circles about 15 cm (6 inches) in diameter. Using a palette knife or rolling pin, transfer to a lightly greased baking sheet.

Work the hazelnuts into the marzipan, then spread some in the centre of each pastry circle.

Peel, quarter and core the apples then slice very thinly. Lay them, slightly overlapping, in a circle around the edge of the pastry, covering the marzipan with the last few slices. Bake in the oven, preheated to 220°C/425°F/gas 7 for about 15–20 minutes.

Meanwhile, make the rum cream by whipping the cream until soft peaks form, then gradually fold in the sugar and rum. Pile into a bowl.

Take the tarts out of the oven. Quickly warm the apricot jam, stirring to ensure smoothness, then glaze the apples lightly.

Serve hot, sprinkled with sugar crystals, and the cream handed round separately.

Use a small saucepan lid to cut out 15 cm (6 inch) diameter circles

Spread a little marzipan-hazelnut mixture in the centre of each circle

To accompany, try a tot of rum, or a glass of Calvados

Fan the apple slices in a circle around the marzipan, then cover the marzipan with two or three slices

Bake in the oven, preheated to 220°C/425°F/gas 7, for 15–20 minutes. Melt the apricot jam, stirring until smooth, then glaze the apples

RHUBARB PIE
TOURTE À LA RHUBARBE

Serves 4

For the pastry:
150 g (5 oz) flour
50 g (2 oz) butter, plus extra for greasing
1 dessert spoon milk
50 g (2 oz) sugar
1 egg yolk
sea salt

For the filling:
450 g (1 lb) rhubarb
1 tablespoon butter
65 g (2½ oz) fine biscuit crumbs
140 g (4½ oz) sugar
1 egg, lightly beaten
1 tablespoon icing sugar

Work all the pastry ingredients together to form a smooth dough, either whizzing everything in a food processor (only a pinch of salt is needed), or by hand in a large mixing bowl. Roll into a ball, wrap in cling film, and chill for about 30 minutes.

Knead the dough again briefly then roll out thinly on a floured surface. Line the base and sides of a buttered pie dish, using two-thirds of the pastry.

Peel the rhubarb and cut into 5 cm (2 inch) lengths. Melt the butter then, off the heat, mix in the biscuit crumbs and sugar and sprinkle half the crumbs over the base of the pie. Fill with the rhubarb and top with the rest of the crumbs.

Knead the remaining pastry into a ball, again roll out thinly and, with the help of the rolling pin, place it over the pie. Remove any excess pastry with the rolling pin. Brush the top of the pie with beaten egg and prick several times with a fork to allow the steam to escape. Bake in the oven, preheated to 220°C/425°F/gas 7, for about 25 minutes, until golden.

Dredge the pie with icing sugar, cut into portions and serve hot.

Spread half the biscuit crumbs evenly over the base of the pie

Cover with the rhubarb and sprinkle on the remaining crumbs

Follow with coffee and fruit eau-de-vie *of choice*

Roll out the rest of the pastry and, using the rolling pin, place it over the filled pie

Roll off and remove excess pastry and brush the top of the pie with beaten egg. Prick several times with a fork to allow the steam to escape

CHEESECAKE FLAN
TARTE AU FROMAGE

Makes 1 × 28 cm (11 inch) or 2 × 15 cm (6 inch) flans

For the pastry:
250 g (9 oz) flour, sifted
sea salt
200 g (7 oz) butter, plus extra for greasing
100 g (3½ oz) sugar
1 teaspoon milk
1 egg

For the filling:
750 g (scant 1¾ lbs) Quark or other low-fat curd cheese
4 egg yolks
150 g (5 oz) sugar
400 ml (14 fl oz) milk
sea salt
grated zest of 1 lemon, lemon well washed first
65 g (2½ oz) cornflour
40 g (1½ oz) flour
4 egg whites

To decorate:
Blackcurrant or strawberry jam

To make the pastry, either whizz all the ingredients together in a food processor to make a smooth dough, or, by hand, work together the flour, a pinch of salt and the butter to the breadcrumbs stage, then add the sugar, milk and egg and knead until smooth. Roll into a ball, wrap in cling film, and chill for about 30 minutes.

For the filling, squeeze the Quark well in muslin to remove excess moisture, then mix thoroughly with the egg yolks, 50 g (2 oz) sugar and the milk. Add a pinch of salt, the lemon zest, cornflour and flour, stirring well until smooth. Whisk the egg whites until stiff, slowly adding the remaining sugar, and fold the egg whites gently into the cheese mixture.

Knead the pastry briefly, roll out thinly on a floured surface, and line the base and sides of a buttered 28 cm (11 inch) flan tin, or two 15 cm (6 inch) tins. Line the pastry with greaseproof paper and weight with dried peas, beans, lentils or rice.

Bake in the oven, preheated to 180°C/350°F/gas 4, for about 10 minutes – the blind baking ensures crisp pastry, and a perfectly flat base. Remove the paper and pulses, and fill the flan(s) with the cheese, then return to the oven and bake for 1 hour. Check after 40 minutes and if the flan(s) are colouring too much, cover with aluminium foil.

Serve hot, with a spoonful of blackcurrant or strawberry jam.

Line the uncooked pastry case(s) with greaseproof paper

Weight the paper with rice or pulses

To accompany, try a sweet white Loire wine, such as Quarts de Chaume, Bonnezeaux or Vouvray

Blind bake at 180°C/350°F/gas 4 for 10 minutes. Remove the paper and pulses

Pour the cheese mixture into the baked pastry case(s), smooth the top and return to the oven for 1 hour

Hot Poppy Cakes with Plum Sorbet

GÂTEAUX CHAUDS AU PAVOT ACCOMPAGNÉ DE SORBET AU RHUM

Serves 4

For the sorbet:

250 g (9 oz) red plums

2 tablespoons caster sugar

5 cm (2 inch) cinnamon stick

2 cloves

grated zest of 1 lemon, lemon well
  washed first

juice of ½ lemon

For the poppy cakes:

100 g (3½ oz) butter, softened, plus
  extra for greasing

100 g (3½ oz) sugar

4 egg yolks

125 g (4 oz) poppy seeds, ground

sea salt

20 g (scant 1 oz) flour, plus extra for
  dusting

20 g (scant 1 oz) breadcrumbs

4 egg whites

For the Arrack cream:

125 ml (4 fl oz) double cream

1 teaspoon Arrack (raki), or substitute
  Pernod or Anisette

1 tablespoon icing sugar

lemon balm or mint leaves, to decorate

Wash and stone the plums, and bring to the boil with the other sorbet ingredients. Simmer, covered, very gently until tender, then sieve, pushing through as much pulp as possible, and leave to cool. Freeze, either in an ice-cream maker, or in a metal bowl in the freezer for 2–3 hours, stirring from time to time to ensure an evenly frozen and very smooth sorbet.

To make the poppy cakes, beat the butter with 75 g (3 oz) sugar until light and fluffy. Gradually add the egg yolks, beating vigorously between each addition, then stir in the poppy seeds, a pinch of salt, the flour and breadcrumbs. Whisk the egg whites until fairly stiff, slowly adding the remaining sugar, and fold gently into the poppy seed mixture.

Lightly butter four individual moulds and sprinkle with flour, shaking out the excess flour before filling the moulds with the poppy cake batter.

Pour about 2.5 cm (1 inch) boiling water into a bain-marie (or roasting pan) lined with kitchen towel or newspaper (this prevents the water bubbling too fiercely). Place the moulds in the water and bake in the oven, preheated to 180°C/350°F/gas 4 for about 40 minutes.

Meanwhile, make the Arrack cream, by whisking the cream until thick but not stiff, then stir in the Arrack and sifted icing sugar. Transfer the sorbet from the freezer to the refrigerator to soften for 30 minutes.

Unmould the poppy cakes and slice while still hot. Fan out the sliced cakes on four plates and make a pool of Arrack cream beside them. Using a tablespoon dipped in hot water, spoon out portions of the plum sorbet and place on the cream. Decorate with a few lemon balm or mint leaves.

Stir the poppy seeds, salt, flour and breadcrumbs into the butter and egg yolk mixture. Fold in the whisked egg whites

Sprinkle the buttered moulds with flour and tip out excess flour

Follow with a fine black China tea, such as Keemun or Yunnan

Place a sheet of kitchen towel in the bain-marie to prevent the water bubbling too fiercely

Fill the moulds with the poppy cake batter, place in the bain-marie and bake in the oven, preheated to 180°C/350°F/gas 4, for about 40 minutes

BATCH BUNS WITH STEWED ELDERBERRIES
PETITS PAINS À LA COMPÔTE DE BAIES DE SUREAU

Serves 4
For the elderberries:

700 g (1½ lbs) elderberries, washed and stalks removed

75 g (3 oz) 'sugar with pectin' (see Note)

4 tablespoons water

zest of 1 lemon and 1 orange, the fruits washed well first

3 plums, stoned

5 cm (2 inch) cinnamon stick

For the buns:

250 g (9 oz) flour, plus extra for dusting

15 g (½ oz) fresh yeast

40 g (1½ oz) sugar

200 ml (7 fl oz) milk, lukewarm

100 g (3½ oz) melted butter

sea salt

grated zest of 1 lemon, lemon well washed first

2 egg yolks

65 g (2½ oz) shelled walnuts, finely chopped

butter for greasing

icing sugar for sprinkling

Put half the elderberries in a pan with the 'sugar with pectin' and the water. Add the thinly pared zests and bring slowly to the boil before adding the plums and cinnamon. Simmer for about 15 minutes, then sieve, pushing through as much pulp as possible, and return to the pan. Add the remaining elderberries and simmer, covered, until tender. Leave to cool and then chill for 1–2 hours.

To make the batch buns, sift the flour into a large mixing bowl, make a well in the centre and into it stir the crumbled yeast with a teaspoon of sugar and a little milk. Cover and leave in a warm place for about 20 minutes until the yeast is frothy and swollen. Then add the remaining milk and sugar, 40 g (1½ oz) butter, a pinch of salt, the lemon zest and egg yolks. Work well together and finally add the walnuts and knead the dough until light and airy.

Cover and leave to rise in a warm, draught-free place, until at least doubled in volume. (Much will depend on the flour, yeast and temperature, but this will probably take 1–2 hours.) Knock back the dough and knead lightly again, then shape into a sausage on a floured board and cut into short lengths.

Pat the pieces into balls, dip into the remaining melted butter (reheated if necessary, it should be warm) and place close together in a buttered, ovenproof dish. Cover with a damp cloth and leave to rise again until nearly doubled in size, about 20 minutes. Then bake in the oven, preheated to 180°C/350°F/gas 4, for about 20 minutes.

Meanwhile quickly reheat the elderberries and pour on to four plates. Once baked, cut the dough into individual buns and place two on each plate of elderberries. Sprinkle with a little icing sugar and serve.

NOTE: Sugar with pectin, made for preserving and jam-making, can be bought at supermarkets.

Shape the dough into a sausage and cut into short lengths

Shape the pieces into small round balls

Accompany with coffee or tea of choice

Using two spoons coat the balls of dough in warm melted butter

Place them close together in a buttered, ovenproof dish. Cover and leave to rise again

CHOCOLATE-ICED NUT BUNS
PETITS PAINS AUX NOIX GLACÉS AU CHOCOLAT

Makes about 45
150 g (5 oz) sugar

150 g (5 oz) ground hazelnuts

150 g (5 oz) ground almonds

100 g (3½ oz) marzipan

*225 g (8 oz) egg white
(approximately 5 × size 2 egg
whites)*

*75 g (3 oz) candied orange peel,
chopped*

25 g (1 oz) flour

2 generous pinches ground cinnamon

1 generous pinch ground nutmeg

2 generous pinches ground cloves

*½ teaspoon baking powder, dissolved
in a few drops water*

*¼ teaspoon grated lemon zest, lemon
washed well first*

*silicone or greaseproof paper cut into
45 rounds 5 cm (2 inches) in
diameter*

For the icing:
250 g (9 oz) dark cooking chocolate

Toast the sugar, hazelnuts and almonds in a frying pan over a low heat, stirring constantly until nicely golden, then cool. Crumble the marzipan and mash with a little egg white until smooth, then gradually work in the cooled nut mixture, the rest of the egg white and the remaining ingredients. Cover the mixture with cling film and leave in the refrigerator or cool place overnight.

Spread the silicone paper rounds on a baking sheet. Shape the nut mixture into small balls, placing each one on a paper, then press lightly to flatten and bake in the oven, preheated to 180°C/350°F/gas 4, for about 15 minutes. Leave to cool on the baking tray.

For the icing, break the chocolate into small pieces, put half in a bowl over a pan of just simmering water. Once melted, stir in the remaining chocolate and melt quickly. Stir briefly to ensure there are no lumps, then chill.

As soon as the chocolate appears creamy in consistency, reheat, again over a pan of hot water, until it reaches a temperature of 32°C/90°F. A thermometer is a necessity here as it is vital not to overheat. Dip the tops of the buns into the chocolate, drain off the excess and place on a rack to dry.

Store in layers, separated by greaseproof paper, in a cake tin with a tightly fitting lid.

Shape the nut mixture into balls, place on silicone paper rounds and flatten lightly

Bake in the oven, preheated to 180°C/ 350°F/gas 4, for about 15 minutes

Accompany with coffee and cognac, if wished

Dip the tops of the buns into the liquid chocolate

Drain off the excess and place on a rack to dry – stand the rack over a tray to catch any drips

STOCKS

Stocks are undoubtedly the bastion of French *haute cuisine* and are an essential ingredient for really good sauces – sauces that will transform an ordinary dish into a gourmet experience. They are time-consuming to make, but the effect is worthwhile since they freeze very well. Stored in small portions, they can then easily be defrosted for use as required. A word of warning, though – when contemplating making a stock, dispel firmly any idea of the traditional 'grandmother's stockpot' eternally bubbling at the side of the stove with all and sundry going into it. A good stock is freshly made from the bones of one creature only, flavoured lightly with herbs and a few vegetables.

WHITE CHICKEN STOCK

Makes about 1.1 litre (2 pints)

1 small bay leaf
1 clove
1 onion, peeled
1 leek, washed and chopped
1 carrot, washed and cut into large dice
1 celery stalk, washed and chopped
2-3 button mushrooms, wiped clean with a damp cloth, sliced
3 tablespoons vegetable oil
1 kg (2 lbs) chicken bones, chopped, or 1 boiling chicken, halved
sea salt
5 white peppercorns

100 ml (3½ fl oz) dry white wine
1.5 litres (2¾ pints) water

Wrap the bay leaf around the onion securing with the clove. Heat the oil in a large pan, add the vegetables, the onion, and the chicken bones or boiling chicken and fry for a few minutes without browning. Season lightly with salt, add the peppercorns and stir in the white wine. Leave to one side until cool.

Then add the water, return to the heat and quickly bring to the boil. Lower the heat and simmer very gently for 2 hours, removing the scum from time to time. Strain the stock and leave to cool, then freeze for use as required.

BROWN CHICKEN STOCK

Makes about 1.1 litre (2 pints)

3 tablespoons vegetable oil
1 kg (2 lbs) chicken giblets and bones (heart, neck, wing tips, etc. – the bones should be raw and chopped)
1 tablespoon tomato purée
1 leek, washed
1 carrot, washed
1 celery stalk, washed
1 shallot, peeled
1 bay leaf
1 onion, peeled
1 clove
1 teaspoon white peppercorns
4 sprigs of parsley
1 small sprig of rosemary
2 tomatoes, quartered

25 g (1 oz) butter
100 ml (3½ oz) sea salt
100 ml (3½ fl oz) white wine
5 tablespoons Madeira
2 litres (3½ pints) water

Brush a large roasting tin with oil, add the chicken giblets and bones and brown in the oven, preheated to 250°C/500°F/gas 9. Stir in the tomato purée and roast for a further 5 minutes.

Coarsely dice the vegetables and secure the bay leaf on to the onion with the clove. Add the vegetables, onion, peppercorns, herbs, tomatoes and butter to the roasting tin and season with salt. Lower the oven heat to 170°C/325°F/gas 3 and cook for a further 15 minutes, stirring from time to time. Remove from the oven, stir in the white wine and Madeira and leave to cool.

Then add the water, bring to the boil on top of the stove and simmer, very gently, for about 3 hours, spooning off scum and fat frequently. Strain, cool, chill, then freeze.

WHITE VEAL STOCK

Makes about 2-2.3 litres (3¹/₂-4 pints)

2 shallots, peeled
1 piece celeriac, peeled
1 leek, washed
2 carrots, peeled
2 kg (4¹/₂ lbs) veal bones and off-cuts, chopped into small pieces
65 g (2¹/₂ oz) butter
sea salt
1 bay leaf
10 white peppercorns
200 ml (7 fl oz) white wine
3 litres (scant 5¹/₂ pints) water

Coarsely dice the vegetables. Heat the butter in a large stock pan (or use 2 very large saucepans), add the vegetables, veal bones and off-cuts and fry for a few minutes without browning. Season lightly with salt, add the bay leaf and peppercorns and stir in the white wine. Remove from the heat and leave to cool.

Add the water, bring quickly to the boil, then simmer very gently for 2 hours. Strain the stock and leave to cool. Chill, then freeze in small portions – it's a good idea to freeze some in ice-cube containers, too, in case only a few tablespoons are needed.

BROWN VEAL STOCK

Makes about 1.1 litres (2 pints)

3 tablespoons vegetable oil
1 kg (2 lbs) veal bones, chopped
2 tablespoons tomato purée
1 celery stalk, trimmed
1 onion, peeled
1 carrot, peeled
4 sprigs of parsley
1 sprig of rosemary
2 bay leaves
2 tomatoes, quartered
10 white peppercorns
sea salt
2 tablespoons butter
100 ml (3¹/₂ fl oz) white wine
5 tablespoons Madeira
2 litres (3¹/₂ pints) water

Brush a roasting tin with the oil, add the veal bones and brown in the oven preheated to 250°C/500°F/gas 9. Stir in the tomato purée and roast for a further 5 minutes.

Coarsely chop the vegetables and add to the veal bones with the herbs, tomatoes and peppercorns. Season with salt, stir in the butter and cook at 170°C/325°F/gas 3 for a further 15 minutes, stirring from time to time. Add the white wine and Madeira, then leave to cool.

Pour in the water, return to the top of the stove and bring to the boil, then simmer very gently for about 3 hours, occasionally removing the fat and scum. Strain, cool, then chill before freezing.

FISH STOCK

Makes about 1 litre (1¾ pints)

500 g (generous 1 lb) bones of
  good-quality sea-fish, e.g. sole or
  turbot
2 shallots, peeled
1 leek, washed
1 piece celeriac, peeled
3 tablespoons vegetable oil
2 slices lemon, lemon washed first
5 white peppercorns
1 sprig of thyme
1 sprig of parsley
1 bay leaf
sea salt
500 ml (18 fl oz) dry white wine
750 ml (27 fl oz) water

Rinse the fish bones in cold water and drain, then finely dice the vegetables. Heat the oil in a large pan, add the vegetables and sweat for a few minutes. Add the lemon slices, peppercorns and herbs and cook for about 2 minutes, then add the fish bones, season lightly with salt and stir in the white wine.

Pour in the water, bring to the boil and then simmer gently for about 25 minutes, removing the scum frequently. Strain the stock and leave to cool. Freeze in small portions for use as required.

With a little flair the art of compiling a menu is easy to learn. The main rule is that a menu should lead up to the main course – from cold to hot, from mild to highly seasoned, from poached to roast. The first course should not be over-filling, but an invitation to the course to come. And if the main course is rich, then the dessert should be light and refreshing. It is important also to remember colour and texture, providing a variety of both as the meal progresses. One other point: the wine for the main course can be served throughout the main part of the meal.

ASPARAGUS
AND
CALVES' BRAIN
SALAD

Sancerre or a New Zealand

Sauvignon Blanc

page 88

·

RUMP STEAKS
BOCUSE

a Merlot-based Bordeaux from

Saint-Émilion or Pomerol

page 42

·

RHUBARB PIE

follow with coffee and

a fruit *eau-de-vie*

page 138

ONION FLAN

Alsace white wine, such as

Pinot Blanc, Pinot Gris

or Riesling

page 106

·

POACHED SADDLE
OF
LAMB

a Médoc Bordeaux from Pauillac,

or a Côte Rôtie

page 54

·

WILLIAM'S PEAR
CHARLOTTE

Asti Spumante or an Alsace *eau-de-vie*

de poire

page 118

TURKEY BREAST FILLETS
IN VEGETABLE JACKETS

a light red Burgundy from the

Hautes Côtes de Beaune, or an Alsace

Pinot Noir

page 74

·

PORK GOULASH

Alsace Gewürztraminer, or

a fine dry cider

page 60

·

GRILLED ORANGES

follow with coffee and the same

liqueur as used in the dessert

page 116

POTATO SOUP
WITH CÈPES

a fine dry Amontillado

or Oloroso sherry

page 98

·

YOUNG PORK LOIN
WITH CABBAGE

a red or white Côtes du Rhône

Villages, or an Anjou red

page 62

·

CURD CHEESE
DUMPLINGS
WITH
APRICOT COMPOTE

a dry apricot *eau-de-vie*

page 112

CALF'S HEAD
WITH TONGUE
IN GREEN SAUCE

a Beaujolais *cru* wine, such as

Moulin-á-Vent or Morgan

page 52

·

STUFFED
SPRING CHICKEN

a full-bodied white Graves or an aged

Australian Sémillon

page 72

·

CHEESECAKE FLAN

Quarts de Chaume,

Bonnezeaux or Vouvray

page 140

ONION AND LEEK SOUP WITH CHEESE

a red or white wine from the
Côtes de Jura

page 104

·

PORK FILLET IN BEER SAUCE

Chinon, Bourgueil or Saumur-
Champigny, or a light Zinfandel from
California

page 58

·

APPLE FRITTERS

Calvados or rum

page 114

MUSSELS IN CURRY SAUCE

Hermitage or a Californian
Chardonnay

page 38

·

HARE ROYALE

Morey-Saint-Denis or
Nuits-Saint-Georges
Premier Cru

page 84

·

CHOCOLATE LEAVES WITH CHESTNUT PURÉE AND HAZELNUT SAUCE

follow with coffee and brandy

page 130

CALVES' SWEETBREAD RAVIOLI

Barbaresco or Valtellina Superiore

page 50

·

STUFFED TURBOT WITH TARRAGON SAUCE

Meursault or Chablis Premier Cru,
or a still Coteaux Champenois

page 24

·

COFFEE ICE CREAM

follow with
coffee and cognac

page 128

RÖSTI WITH PASTRY TOPPING

a dry white Savoie wine, such as
Crépy or Seyssel, or a dry white
Swiss wine, such as Forin or Fendant

page 102

·

GLAZED GAMMON

a light Médoc Bordeaux from
Margaux or Saint-Julien

page 64

·

CHEESE BOARD

STUFFED BAKED POTATOES

Beaujolais Villages or Irouléguy

page 98

·

BRAISED CARP

an Alsace Pinot Gris, or an
old style white Rioja, such as
Marqués de Murrieta
or CUNE's Monopole

page 12

·

FRENCH APPLE TARTS WITH RUM CREAM

Calvados or rum

page 136

STUFFED COURGETTE FLOWERS

a Spätlese from the Mosel or an
English wine, such as Lamberhurst,
Carr Taylor or Pulham

page 92

·

SALMON AND SPINACH LASAGNE

an Australian Chardonnay or a
red Anjou or Gamay de Touraine,
served slightly chilled

page 14

·

HOT POPPY CAKES WITH PLUM SORBET

follow with a fine black China tea

page 142

POTATO FRITTERS WITH SNAILS

Chablis, or an Australian
Rhine Riesling

page 100

·

POACHED HADDOCK WITH MUSTARD BUTTER

Gewürztraminer or
Traminer from Alto Adige

page 28

·

CRÊPES BOCUSE

follow with coffee and the
same liqueur as used
in the dessert

page 126

ICED PEPPER SOUP WITH LANGOUSTINES

Côtes de Provence rosé, or
a Portuguese Vinho Verde

page 32

·

BRAISED BEEF AND VEGETABLES

Châteauneuf-du-Pape
or Lirac

page 46

·

BATCH BUNS WITH STEWED ELDERBERRIES

coffee or tea

page 144

SALTED HERRINGS IN ASPIC WITH HERB SAUCE

chilled Fino sherry, or a strong,
dry Normandy cider

page 30

·

POACHED FILLET OF BEEF

a Loire red from Chinon
or Bourgueil, or a Médoc such as
Margaux or St Julien

page 44

·

CHOCOLATE-ICED NUT BUNS

cognac and coffee

page 146

CHEESE AND SPINACH TART

a red or white wine from the Loire
valley or from Switzerland

page 94

·

RED MULLET WITH A BASIL DRESSING

a rosé wine
or a chilled Fino sherry

page 22

·

APRICOT AND YOGHURT CREAMS

Muscat de Beaumes de Venise
or Muscat de Lunel

page 110

LOBSTER AND FRESH PEA SOUP

Muscadet de Sèvre-et-Maine *sur lie,*
or a Madeira such as Extra Reserve
Sercial or Verdelho

page 34

·

DUCK A L'ORANGE

an Italian Barbera or a
Californian Zinfandel

page 76

·

STUFFED HAZELNUT CRÊPES

a sweet Sauternes or Monbazillac,
or an Alsace
eau-de-vie de poire

page 124

SCALLOPS IN SORREL SAUCE

Quincy or Pouilly Fumé

page 36

·

CHICKEN IN RED WINE

a red Burgundy from the
Côte Chalonnaise, such as
Mercurey or Givry

page 70

·

RUM PUDDING WITH PEARS IN RED WINE

rum or Vintage
Character port

page 120

INDEX

Y